Editor
Eric Migliaccio

Editorial Project Manager
Ina Massler Levin, M.A.

Editor in Chief
Sharon Coan, M.S. Ed.

Illustrator
Ben DeSoto

Cover Artist
Jessica Orlando

Art Coordinator
Denice Adorno

Creative Director
Richard D'Sa

Imaging
Alfred Lau
James Edward Grace

Product Manager
Phil Garcia

Publishers
Rachelle Cracchiolo, M.S. Ed.
Mary Dupuy Smith, M.S. Ed.

Enhancing Writing with Visuals

Grades 3–5

Written by

Kathleen N. Kopp, M.S. Ed.

Teacher Created Materials, Inc.
6421 Industry Way
Westminster, CA 92683
www.teachercreated.com
ISBN-1-57690-993-X

©2000 Teacher Created Materials, Inc.
Made in U.S.A.

Table of Contents

Activities: From Head to Toe—The Longest Story—Oh, Clam Up!—Around the Solar System—The Day Santa's Shape Changed—Oh, What a Scene!—In the Beginning—The Loud Noise—"Just So"—The Airplane Ride—The Great Easter Egg Hunt—Who Said That?—Story Props—The Mystery of the . . .—The Sweetest Story—The Annoying Fly

Activities: Yum, Yum!—All About Me—How To . . .—Futuristic Society—Just for You, Johnny Appleseed!—Three Cheers for the Red, White, and Blue!—Famous People—Meet My Friend—The Ultimate Ice-Cream Sundae—The Graph Club—Body Systems—Country Reports—The Pyramids—Scientifically Speaking

Activities: On the Playground—Futuristic Fun Time—Current Events—The Best Thanksgiving Dinner Ever—The Reluctant Leprechaun—Persuasive Advertising—But, Mom!!!—Dear Mr. President—Healthy Eating, Healthy Day—Keys to Good Test Taking—A Good Book, Anyone?—Nursery Rhyme Time—Learn to Conserve!—From the Ground Up—Stadium Proposal

Activities: Magazine Mania—Making News—A Piece of Realia—About Time—A Welcome Burial—Another World—Sight Unseen—Love Is In the Air—Alliteration ABC—Figuratively Speaking—Angles and Such—Mystery Object—Radical Rocks—Unequivocally News—Nature Takes a Hike

Activities: At the Ballgame—Out of the Box—Bang!—Birds of a Feather—Spring—Happiness Is Haiku—A Shapely Poem—A Card For All Occasions—Kites—All About Autumn—Native Expressions—At War

Introduction

Teaching students to write well has become one of our nation's highest priorities in education. Some states now require students to demonstrate competency in writing through the administration of a formal writing assessment; and drawings, diagrams, and colorful pages aren't exactly what the readers are looking for when they score students' papers. They focus more on content and organization and wish to see no frills, fancies, or other distracting features—however complimentary to the text they may be. Some states may not have a writing assessment but require teachers to instruct specific benchmarks related to writing. Other states may not have strict criteria in regards to writing, but writing is part of a well-rounded curriculum.

Regardless of the state in which you teach, your objective is the same: instruct and encourage students to write effectively. Whether you are focused on form and content or are free to teach writing as you see fit, this book offers ideas and activities that allow students to apply effective writing skills in a more artistic and visually appealing manner.

The book is divided into five main categories. Included are ideas for narrative, expository, persuasive, descriptive, and poetry writing. Some of the activities are integrated to correspond with topics and subjects you may already be studying in class. Others suggest a writing activity to go along with a holiday theme. Still others are generic in nature and may be used by students across grade levels.

Each activity is first described for the teacher. This description includes prewriting activities, the steps involved in the assignment, and publishing ideas for when the students finish. Some even offer follow-up ideas for those of you who choose to provide extensions whenever necessary. Most of the activities are followed up with student activity pages. Check the materials list following each teacher explanation to see if a student page is provided. These student activity pages are designed to stand alone, if needed. Most allow for free writing by the students without a lot of prompting and filling-in. In this way, the teacher may check to be sure the students are applying their writing form and content skills to miscellaneous tasks.

These activities are writing activities first and are enhanced by visuals second. Visual enhancers may be as simple as using a different lettering or font or by using colored or textured paper; or they may be more complicated, such as completing an art project that may take a couple of days to finish. Others include, but are not limited to, featuring illustrations, pictures, graphs, or charts; utilizing shapes (both two- and three-dimensional) to brainstorm ideas and to use within the actual writing; providing accompaniments, such as artwork, dioramas, mobiles, posters, etc.; and creating professional-looking documents with word-processing and multimedia programs.

And remember, whatever the task, never settle for your students' second best. Enhancing a writing project with visuals is a lot more fun than just writing. The ideas set forth in this publication may even inspire you to think of creative ways to help turn any ordinary writing assignment into a visually appealing and deceptively fun project.

Get ready, get set, write!

Standards for Writing
Grades 3–5

Accompanying the major activities of this book will be references to the basic standards and benchmarks for writing that will be met by successful performance of the activities. Each specific standard and benchmark will be referred to by the appropriate letter and number from the following collection. For example, a basic standard and benchmark identified as **1A** would be as follows:

> **Standard 1:** Demonstrates competence in the general skills and strategies of the writing process
>
> **Benchmark A:** Prewriting: Uses prewriting strategies to plan written work (e.g., uses graphic organizers, story maps, and webs; groups related ideas; takes notes; brainstorms ideas)

A basic standard and benchmark identified as **4B** would be as follows:

> **Standard 4:** Gathers and uses information for research purposes
>
> **Benchmark B:** Uses encyclopedias to gather information for research topics

Clearly, some activities will address more than one standard. Moreover, since there is a rich supply of activities included in this book, some will overlap in the skills they address; and some, of course, will not address every single benchmark within a given standard. Therefore, when you see these standards referenced in the activities, refer to this section for complete descriptions.

Although virtually every state has published its own standards and every subject area maintains its own lists, there is surprising commonality among these various sources. For the purposes of this book, we have elected to use the collection of standards synthesized by John S. Kendall and Robert J. Marzano in their book *Content Knowledge: A Compendium of Standards and Benchmarks for K–12 Education* (Second Edition, 1997) as illustrative of what students at various grade levels should know and be able to do. The book is published jointly by McREL (Mid-continent Regional Educational Laboratory, Inc.) and ASCD (Association for Supervision and Curriculum Development). (Used by permission of McREL.)

Language Arts Standards

1. Demonstrates competence in the general skills and strategies of the writing process

2. Demonstrates competence in the stylistic and rhetorical aspects of writing

3. Uses grammatical and mechanical conventions in written compositions

4. Gathers and uses information for research purposes

Standards for Writing
Grades 3–5 *(cont.)*

Level II (Grades 3–5)

> **1. Demonstrates competence in the general skills and strategies of the writing process**

A. Prewriting: Uses prewriting strategies to plan written work (e.g., uses graphic organizers, story maps, and webs; groups related ideas; takes notes; brainstorms ideas)

B. Drafting and Revising: Uses strategies to draft and revise written work (e.g., elaborates on a central idea; writes with attention to voice, audience, word choice, tone, and imagery; uses paragraphs to develop separate ideas)

C. Editing and Publishing: Uses strategies to edit and publish written work (e.g., edits for grammar, punctuation, capitalization, and spelling at a developmentally-appropriate level; considers page format [paragraphs, margins, indentations, titles]; selects presentation format; incorporates photos, illustrations, charts, and graphs)

D. Evaluates own and others' writing (e.g., identifies the best features of a piece of writing, determines how own writing achieves its purposes, asks for feedback, responds to classmates' writing)

E. Writes stories or essays that show awareness of intended audience

F. Writes stories or essays that convey an intended purpose (e.g., to record ideas, to describe, to explain)

G. Writes expository compositions (e.g., identifies and stays on the topic; develops the topic with simple facts, details, examples, and explanations; excludes extraneous and inappropriate information)

H. Writes narrative accounts (e.g., engages the reader by establishing a context and otherwise creates an organizational structure that balances and unifies all narrative aspects of the story; uses sensory details and concrete language to develop plot and character; uses a range of strategies such as dialogue and tension or suspense)

I. Writes autobiographical compositions (e.g., provides a context within which the incident occurs, uses simple narrative strategies, provides some insight into why this incident is memorable)

Standards for Writing
Grades 3–5 *(cont.)*

J. Writes expressive compositions (e.g., expresses ideas, reflections, and observations; uses an individual, authentic voice; uses narrative strategies, relevant details, and ideas that enable the reader to imagine the world of the event or experience)

K. Writes in response to literature (e.g., advances judgements; supports judgements with references to the text, other works, other authors, nonprint media, and personal knowledge)

L. Writes personal letters (e.g., includes the date, address, greeting, and closing; addresses envelopes)

2. Demonstrates competence in the stylistic and rhetorical aspects of writing

A. Uses descriptive language that clarifies and enhances ideas (e.g., describes familiar people, places, or objects)

B. Uses paragraph form in writing (e.g., indents the first word of a paragraph, uses topic sentences, recognizes a paragraph as a group of sentences about one main idea, writes several related paragraphs)

C. Uses a variety of sentence structures

3. Uses grammatical and mechanical conventions in written compositions

A. Writes in cursive

B. Uses exclamatory and imperative sentences in written compositions

C. Uses pronouns in written compositions (e.g., substitutes pronouns for nouns)

D. Uses nouns in written compositions (e.g., uses plural and singular naming words; forms regular and irregular plurals of nouns; uses common and proper nouns; uses nouns as subjects)

E. Uses verbs in written compositions (e.g., uses a wide variety of action verbs, past and present verb tenses, simple tenses, forms of regular verbs, verbs agree with subjects)

F. Uses adjectives in written compositions (e.g., indefinite, numerical, predicate adjectives)

G. Uses adverbs in written compositions (e.g., to make comparisons)

H. Uses coordinating conjunctions in written compositions (e.g., links ideas using connecting words)

I. Uses negatives in written compositions (e.g., avoids double negatives)

Standards for Writing
Grades 3-5 *(cont.)*

J. Uses conventions of spelling in written compositions (e.g., spells high-frequency, commonly misspelled words from appropriate grade-level list; uses a dictionary and other resources to spell words; uses initial consonant substitution to spell related words; uses vowel combinations for correct spelling)

K. Uses conventions of capitalization in written compositions (e.g., titles of people; proper nouns [names of towns, cities, counties, and states; days of the week; months of the year; names of streets; names of countries; holidays]; first word of direct quotations; heading, salutation, and closing of a letter)

L. Uses conventions of punctuation in written compositions (e.g., uses periods after imperative sentences and in initials, abbreviations, and titles before names; uses commas in dates and addresses and after greetings and closings in a letter; uses apostrophes in contractions and possessive nouns; uses quotation marks around titles and with direct quotations; uses a colon between hours and minutes)

4. Gathers and uses information for research purposes

A. Uses a variety of strategies to identify topics to investigate (e.g., brainstorms, lists questions, uses idea webs)

B. Uses encyclopedias to gather information for research topics

C. Uses dictionaries to gather information for research topics

D. Uses key words, indexes, cross-references, and letters on volumes to find information for research topics

E. Uses multiple representations of information (e.g., maps, charts, photos) to find information for research topics

F. Uses graphic organizers (e.g., notes, charts, graphs) to gather and record information for research topics

G. Compiles information into written reports or summaries

Narrative Writing

From Head to Toe

The Longest Story

Oh, Clam Up!

Around the Solar System

The Day Santa's Shape Changed

Oh, What a Scene!

In the Beginning

The Loud Noise

"Just So"

The Airplane Ride

The Great Easter Egg Hunt

Who Said That?

Story Props

The Mystery of the . . .

The Sweetest Story

The Annoying Fly

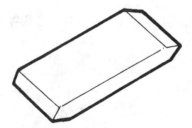

From Head to Toe

No matter what kind of paper students use to write their stories, they may dress them up with simple, eye-catching artwork centered around the theme of their stories. For example, they may write a story about choosing a watermelon from a watermelon patch and sandwich it between a watermelon top and bottom cut from green construction paper. Of course, the watermelon wouldn't be complete without adding two or three "vines" which can be made by curling green construction paper around a pencil and securing one end to a side of the watermelon.

Students may wish to write a scary story on a large sheet of gray construction paper (or white drawing paper colored with a gray crayon) which has been cut to resemble a tombstone. (Don't forget the "R.I.P." towards the top!)

Writing a story about a silly person? Students may attach a silly head peeking over the top of their story and goofy shoes secured to the bottom.

The possibilities are endless. The prompts on pages 10–14 offer suggestions for visual enhancers. Better yet, let the students be their own designers. Allow them to think of original ways to embellish their own otherwise ordinary stories! And these creations make excellent displays on any bulletin board or drab hallway. (See examples on page 15.)

Materials

"In the Watermelon Patch" (page 10)

- large sheet of green construction paper
- light green crayon
- scissors
- glue

"Across the Graveyard" (page 11)

- large sheet of white drawing paper
- gray crayon
- glue

"The Silliest Person" (page 12)

- drawing and construction paper
- crayons or markers
- yarn
- glue

"The Wild Beast" (page 13)

- miscellaneous art supplies
- glue

"My Pet Mouse Is Lost!" (page 14)

- brown and pink construction paper
- brown pipe cleaners
- brown yarn
- tape and/or glue

Name _____ Date _____

From Head to Toe *(cont.)*

In the Watermelon Patch

Directions: Write a story to tell about a time your family visited a watermelon patch to select a fresh watermelon for a special occasion. Use the lines below. Continue on a separate sheet of paper, if needed. Glue any additional story sheets to the bottom of this page.

Create a watermelon border for your story:

❑ Use green construction paper. Cut an oblong shape similar to a watermelon out of the paper.

❑ Use a light green crayon to add lines to the outside rind of the watermelon.

❑ Cut your melon in half in a zigzag pattern across the middle of the rind.

❑ Glue the top half of the melon to the top of your story and the bottom half at the end of your story.

❑ Cut two or three thin strips of green contruction paper. Curl the strips of paper by wrapping them around a pencil. Attach the "vines" to one end of your watermelon.

_____

_____

_____

_____

_____

_____

_____

_____

_____

_____

From Head to Toe *(cont.)*

Across the Graveyard

Directions: Graveyards can seem like scary places, especially on a foggy night. Write about what happens when you take a shortcut home across a graveyard one foggy night. Use the lines below. Continue on a separate sheet of paper, if needed. Glue any additional story sheets to the bottom of this page.

Create a headstone border for your story:

❑ Cut a tombstone shape from large white construction paper.

❑ Use the side of a crayon to color the tombstone gray.

❑ Include an "R.I.P." towards the top of the tombstone in a darker gray or black color.

❑ Glue your graveyard story to the middle and bottom of the tombstone. It's okay if it hangs below the bottom of the grave marker.

_____

_____

_____

_____

_____

_____

_____

_____

_____

_____

_____

_____

_____

_____

_____

Name _____ Date _____

From Head to Toe (cont.)

The Silliest Person

Directions: Do you know a particularly silly person? Write a story telling about a time that person did something really goofy. Use the lines below. Continue on a separate sheet of paper, if needed. Glue any additional story sheets to the bottom of this page.

Make your story look like a silly person:

❑ Use drawing paper to create the top half of this person's face from the nose up. Use yarn for hair. Attach the image of the face to the front edge of the top of your story.

❑ Cut four long, thin strips of colored construction paper for arms and legs. Fold them accordion-style. Glue the edges to the back side of your paper. The arms should be glued on the sides of the story, the legs on the bottom of the story.

❑ Make hands and feet and glue them to the ends of the arms and legs.

_____

_____

_____

_____

_____

_____

_____

_____

_____

_____

_____

_____

_____

Name _____ Date _____

From Head to Toe (cont.)

The Wild Beast

Directions: What would you do if you ran into a wild animal while walking through the woods or jungle? Tell a story about your experience. Use the lines below. Continue on a separate sheet of paper, if needed. Glue any additional story sheets to the bottom of this page.

Decorate your story to look like the wild animal in your story:

❑ Use construction paper, paper plates, yarn, crayons, and other art supplies to create your animal image. For example, if you wrote about a tiger, cut orange construction paper into the shape of a tail and draw the black stripes with a crayon or marker. Glue the tail to one side of your story. A lion story might have a large mane made from large yellow paper and yellow yarn surrounding the entire page.

_____

_____

_____

_____

_____

_____

_____

_____

_____

_____

_____

_____

_____

_____

_____

_____

From Head to Toe (cont.)

My Pet Mouse Is Lost!

Directions: People sometimes become frantic when small animals escape their cages. What if your pet mouse escaped? Write a story about your search to find him. Use the lines below. Continue on a separate sheet of paper, if needed. Glue any additional story sheets to the bottom of this page.

Decorate your story with a mouse's ears, whiskers, and tail:

❏ Use brown and pink construction paper to make two large mouse ears. Attach them to the top of your story.

❏ Attach pipe cleaners to each side of your story to represent whiskers.

❏ For the tail, attach a long piece of brown yarn to the bottom of your story.

_____

_____

_____

_____

_____

_____

_____

_____

_____

_____

_____

_____

_____

_____

_____

_____

From Head to Toe (cont.)
Bulletin Board Examples

The Longest Story

Some days seem like they'll never end. Students use the never-ending pattern on page 17 to tell a tale about a day they thought would never end. Allow time for students to share their tales. Whose seems the longest? Secure all the stories end-to-end down a hallway or around the room for a never-ending display.

Materials

- activity sheet (page 17)
- glue
- scissors

Oh, Clam Up!

Who wouldn't want their every wish to come true? Students tell a tale about the day they find a magical clam who grants them one wish. When finished, they create a large clam shape in which to tuck their tales. Students decorate and cut out two samples of the clam shape on page 18. They secure the two inside edges so that the decorated sides both face out when the clam is closed. Then they fold their stories for safe keeping inside their clam cutouts, similar to a pearl.

Materials

- writing paper
- two copies of the clam pattern (page 18)
- glue or tape

Around the Solar System

Interplanetary travel may still be in our future, but students can envision a journey through space as they create an original tale about a trip through our solar system. Students follow the directions on page 19 to create a model of the planets upon which to write their stories. Suspend the finished products from the ceiling or tack them up on a bulletin board for a real display that's out of this world!

Materials

- activity sheet (page 19)
- yarn or string
- glue or tape
- construction paper (two 6" sheets, five 4" sheets, two 2" sheets)

Name _____   Date _____

The Longest Story

Directions: Have you ever thought a bad day would never come to an end? Write a story about your longest day. Begin your story at the beginning of the ruler. Continue until you have finished your story. Copy and cut out all the ruler edges you need. Tape or glue them together to make one looooong story!

Tab

The Magical Clam

Directions: On separate paper, write a story about the day you found a magical clam who granted you one wish. Hide your story where clams keep their pearls by coloring and cutting out the two clam patterns below. Place them together so the outside edges match. Glue or tape the back edges of the clam together. Unfold the clam. Fold your story into a small square and place it between the two clamshells. Now that's a gem of a story!

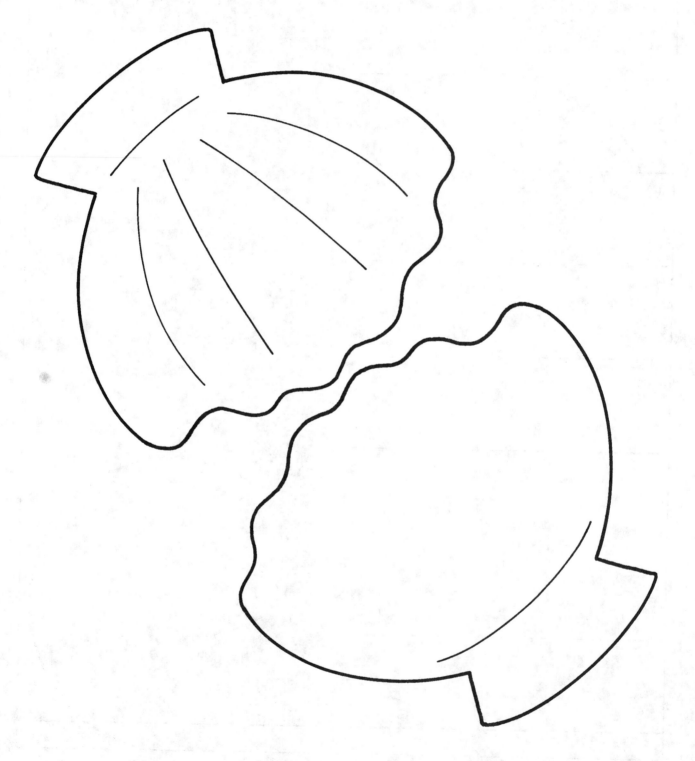

Name _____ Date _____

Around the Solar System

Directions: Think about what might happen on an adventure trip through our solar system. Use the three different sizes of circles to represent the different planets. Then write your story beginning on Mercury and ending on Pluto. Attach the planets in order with yarn or string.

- Mercury (small)
- Venus (medium)
- Earth (medium)

- Mars (small)
- Jupiter (large)
- Saturn (large)

- Uranus (medium)
- Neptune (medium)
- Pluto (small)

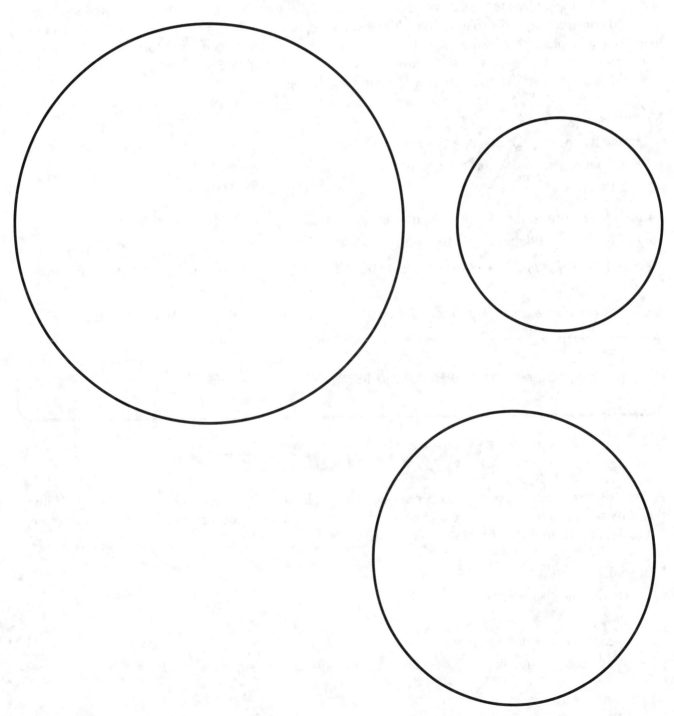

The Day Santa's Shape Changed

We are all familiar with the roly-poly image of the American Santa Claus. But are the students aware of the many shapes, sizes, and forms Santa has around the world? For example, in the mountains of Switzerland, Santa (called Christkindl) has wings and rides a sleigh pulled by reindeer. But in Korea, Santa wears a hat and carries his gifts in a wicker basket on his back. (For more information, see the resources listed below.) Following a study of Santas from other countries, discuss their various shapes and sizes and then have students create an original shape for their Santa by cutting a random shape from red construction paper. They then add a head (complete with hat), mittens, and boots to make their Santa complete. Following their creation, students write a story using the story starter on page 21 or one of their own. Create a class book of the Santas or buddy up with a younger class and have the students share their stories and Santas with younger children.

Materials

- activity sheet (page 21)
- red, white, and black construction paper
- cotton
- glue
- scissors
- crayons or markers

Santa Claus Around the World Resource Books

Santa Claus Around the World by Lisl Weil

Merry Christmas: Children at Christmastime Around the World by Satomi Ichikawa (text by Robina Beckles Willson)

A Christmas Celebration: Traditions and Customs from Around the World by Pamela Kennedy

Oh, What a Scene!

A story's setting can set the stage for a profound story, taking the ordinary to the extraordinary. With this activity students center a story around a captivating setting, then decorate the borders of their story with vibrant artwork to really set the story apart.

Materials

- activity sheet (page 22)
- glue
- large sheet of construction paper
- paints, construction paper, tissue paper, crayons, or other art supplies

The Day Santa's Shape Changed

Directions: What if Santa Claus had a bizarre shape? Use red construction paper to cut a random shape to make Santa's body. Then use white, red, and black construction paper; cotton; and crayons to make his face, hat, mittens, and boots.

Now use the story starter below to write a story about the day Santa's shape changed. Use additional writing paper, if needed. Or you may wish to think of your own beginning and use separate paper to write your story.

Christmas Eve had finally arrived! Santa began his long journey delivering presents to all the boys and girls around the world. But wait! What was that strange light up ahead? Before Santa could act, his lead reindeer had flown into a space warp. When Santa emerged on the other side, his shape had changed! He no longer looked like a big, jolly man; instead he looked like a _____

_____

_____

_____

_____

_____

_____

_____

_____

_____

_____

_____

_____

_____

_____

Name _____   Date _____

Oh, What a Scene!

Directions: The setting of a story can be one of its most important elements. Think for a moment about the most outrageous scene you can imagine for your original story: outer space? an eerie cave? the jungle? Next, decide who will be in your story. Then think of a problem that might occur within the setting you selected. Use the lines below to write your story. Continue it on a separate sheet of paper, if needed.

After you've finished, glue the story in the center of a large sheet of construction paper. Use art materials such as tissue paper, construction paper, paints, or crayons to illustrate the setting around the outside of your story.

_____

_____

_____

_____

_____

_____

_____

_____

_____

_____

_____

_____

_____

_____

_____

_____

_____

_____

In the Beginning

When word processing, encourage students to experiment with fonts and sizes to begin their stories with large, gothic letters; enlarged, colored letters; or enlarged, outlined letters. (See the student activities on pages 24–28.) Post the students' published works on a bulletin board display.

Remember, too, that some desktop publishing programs allow students options when beginning paragraphs.

Materials

- word-processing or desktop-publishing software
- "Once Upon a Time" (page 24)
- "A Medieval Story" (page 25)
- "The Signing of the Declaration of Independence" (page 26)
- "On Yonder Prairie" (page 27)
- "Oh, Horrors!" (page 28)

Standards and Benchmarks: 1E, 1F, 1H, 2A, 2B, 2C

The Loud Noise

Following the same idea as in "In the Beginning" above, have students use all capital letters or boldface to stress certain words within their writings. The student activity sheet on page 29 will help get the students started. Some word-processing and desktop-publishing programs even allow the typist to assign special effects to letters, words, and sentences such as "sparkling" or "blinking." Refer to your program's user's manual for more detailed explanations. When sharing the students' work, attach an overhead monitor or large projection screen to your computer so the students may share their "special effects" stories with the class.

Materials

- student activity sheet (page 29)
- word-processing or desktop-publishing software

Name _____   Date _____

In the Beginning *(cont.)*

Once Upon a Time

Directions: Write your own fairy tale. Think of the characters, setting, problem, and events that will take place leading up to the conflict resolution. Begin your story with "Once upon a time. . . ." Draw a fancy letter "O" in the box to begin your story.

```
┌──────────┐
│          │
│          │
│          │
│          │
│          │
└──────────┘ _____
```

_____

_____

_____

_____

_____

_____

_____

_____

_____

_____

_____

_____

_____

_____

_____

_____

_____

Name _____ Date _____

In the Beginning *(cont.)*
A Medieval Story

Directions: Write a story that takes place during medieval times. You might want to include dragons, knights, damsels in distress, castles, magical beings, or other medieval-like characters and settings. Next think about the problem that occurs in your story and the events that lead up to the conflict resolution. Begin your story by writing a fancy beginning letter in the box.

In the Beginning (cont.)

The Signing of the Declaration of Independence

Directions: Write a story to tell what might have happened during the signing of the Declaration of Independence. Include characters who were really there as well as some that are fictional. Next, think about a problem that might have occurred during this historic event. Include events that lead up to the conflict resolution. Begin your story by writing a fancy beginning letter in the box.

In the Beginning *(cont.)*

On Yonder Prairie

Directions: Write a story that takes place as a family journeys westward in the 1800s. Develop your characters and establish the setting. Consider a problem that occurs as this family travels the trail as well as events that lead up to the conflict resolution. Begin your story by writing a fancy beginning letter in the box.

In the Beginning (cont.)

Oh, Horrors!

Directions: Write a spooky story. Include at least one scary character and set the story in a spooky setting. Then decide on a problem that occurs in your story and the events that lead up to the conflict resolution. Begin your story by writing a fancy beginning letter in the box.

The Loud Noise

Directions: Write a story about a time when you heard a loud noise. When you describe the noise, be sure to write the action sound in either ALL CAPITAL LETTERS or in bold. A sample story has been started for you. You may continue this story or think up your own beginning.

Example:

One afternoon after school, my friend Charlie and I were out back jumping on the trampoline when all of a sudden, WHOOOOOOSH! We heard a sound like a giant horsefly buzzing overhead. Before we could even look up to see what had flown above the trees, CRASH! BANG! Something had fallen to the ground and tumbled through the trees. Charlie and I ran towards the sound to see what it was. We couldn't believe our eyes!

"Just So"

Rudyard Kipling is best known for his "Just So" stories, tales that explain the extraordinary. Some better known ones are "How the Camel Got Its Hump" and "How the Leopard Got Its Spots." After listening to or reading some of his stories, students can develop their own tales to help explain some animals' oddities, such as "How the Giraffe Got Its Neck" or "How the Turtle Got Its Shell." To visually enhance their work, enlarge the shape patterns on pages 31 and 32 to allow students to write their stories inside the animals' shapes. (In the case of the zebra, have students print their stories on white paper and paste them onto the zebra's body.) Following their writing, students may color or decorate their animals. Create a bulletin board display with a jungle-like background entitled "And It Happened Just So."

Materials

- "Just So" stories by Rudyard Kipling
- enlarged patterns on pages 31 and 32

Sample Titles for Original "Just So" Stories

- ❏ "How the Giraffe Got Its Neck"
- ❏ "How the Turtle Got Its Shell"
- ❏ "How the Horse Got Its Tail"
- ❏ "How the Moose Got Its Antlers"

- ❏ "How the Pig Got Its Squeal"
- ❏ "How the Anteater Got Its Nose"
- ❏ "How the Zebra Got Its Stripes"
- ❏ "How the Penguin Got Its Waddle"

The Airplane Ride

Airplanes are supposed to be the safest form of travel. But not all flights are without problems. Students write an original narrative detailing some problem with an aircraft in flight, then fold their papers into the shape of a paper airplane and "fly" it to a friend across the room to share. Use the instructions on page 33 to demonstrate how to fold a paper airplane.

Materials

- activity sheet (page 33)
- paper airplane books (optional)

Paper Airplane Resources

Super Paper Airplanes by Norman Schmidt

How to Have Fun with Paper by Stewart Cowley

Kid's Paper Airplane Book by Ken Blackburn and Jeff Lammers

Amazing Paper Airplanes by Edmund Hui, Ph. D.

The Best Paper Airplanes You'll Ever Fly by the editors of *Klutz*

"Just So" (cont.)
Animal Shape Patterns

"Just So" (cont.)
Animal Shape Patterns

The Airplane Ride

Directions: Flying in an airplane can be an exciting (or frightening) experience, especially when something goes wrong. Think about what might happen on an airplane that has some sort of trouble in the middle of its flight. Now tell a story about this experience. Write your story on a separate piece of paper.

When you're finished, fold your paper into a paper airplane. Use the instructions below to assist you in making your paper airplane.

How to Make a Paper Airplane

1. Fold paper in half. Make a crease.

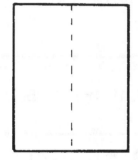

4. Now fold the paper in half.

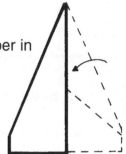

2. Fold each top corner in toward the middle.

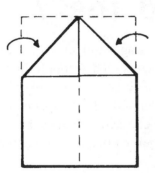

5. Fold the sides down about halfway. These are the wings.

3. Fold each top corner further down toward the middle this time.

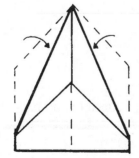

6. Level the wings out straight. Get ready for takeoff!

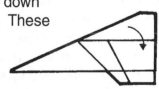

Standards and Benchmarks: 1E, 1F, 1H, 2A, 2B, 2C

The Great Easter Egg Hunt

Students will enjoy sharing a favorite egg-hunt tale by hiding it within a decorated egg. Share a favorite Easter egg hunt experience or other springtime story; then have students write their own story on the egg pattern on page 35. Cut out the egg-shaped story and trace around it onto white construction paper. The blank egg is then decorated, cut out, and cut down the middle in a whimsical pattern. Students place their egg stories underneath the egg cutout and secure them around the outside edge with a light line of glue. Allow time for students to read their stories to a partner or the class before taking them home to post on the refrigerator.

Materials

- activity sheet (page 35)
- white construction paper
- scissors
- glue

Standards and Benchmarks: 1E, 1F, 1H, 2A, 2B, 2C, 3L

Who Said That?

Most stories benefit from the use of dialogue. To encourage students to use dialogue in their narratives, have them write a story with no more than three characters. They should include dialogue in their stories, then practice telling their stories with the use of finger puppets. Students may use the patterns on page 36 as models for their finger puppets. They decorate their puppets to resemble their characters, then tell their stories to a classmate. When one of the characters speaks, he moves that finger up and down to indicate that he is talking. The following scenarios may help students get started:

- ❑ Two aliens are in a spaceship nearing Earth.
- ❑ Two bank robbers try to hold up a bank teller.
- ❑ On the playground, you and a friend are approached by a bully.

Materials

- writing paper
- finger puppet pattern (3) on page 36

Innovation on a good idea

For added practice, have students hunt through the funny pages from your local newspaper and cut out a strip of their choice along with the existing dialogue from the speech bubbles. Then they create their own fanciful strip by gluing down the comic boxes onto another sheet of paper and writing their own dialogue in the blank speech bubbles. Post the students' work on a bulletin board entitled "Funny You Should Say That!"

The Great Easter Egg Hunt

Directions: Write a story to tell what happened during an Easter egg hunt, or think of a springtime story of your own to tell. Use the egg shape below to write your story.

When you're finished, cut out your story. Trace the egg shape onto a sheet of white construction paper. Decorate the egg. Cut it out and make a zigzag or wavy cut down the center. Use a light amount of glue around the outside of the egg and glue it to the top of your story. Fold back the edges so your story peeks out from behind the decorated egg.

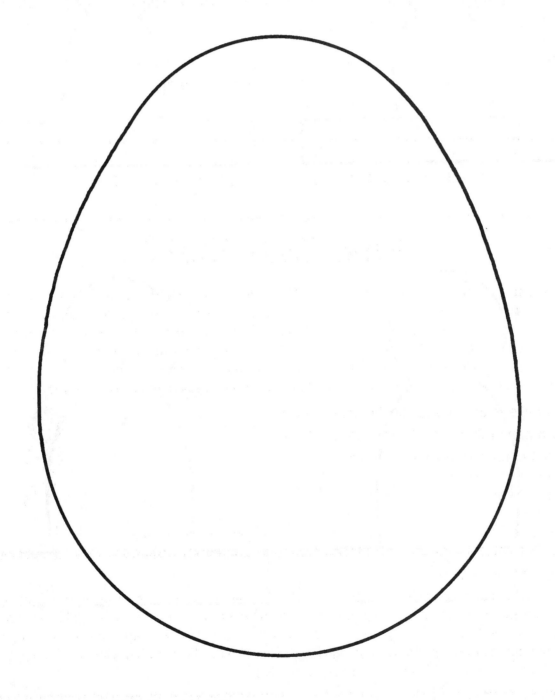

Who Said That?

Directions: Use the finger puppet patterns below with "Who Said That?" on page 34. Illustrate and cut out two or three puppets to use with your dialogue narratives.

Story Props

Students may wish to write an original story that includes some simple prop or item related to their tale. To demonstrate, read *The Talking Eggs* by Robert D. San Souci or *The Rainbow Fish* by Marcus Pfister. Ask the students if they were going to read either of these stories to a younger student, what kind of simple prop could they include to entice the young learner's interest in the story? To introduce *The Talking Eggs*, they may display a plain white egg-shaped piece of paper and a decorated egg-shaped piece of paper. To introduce *The Rainbow Fish*, their prop might be as simple as a piece of tin foil folded to resemble a shiny fish scale. As students finish one of their stories intended for a younger student, challenge them to create simple props to accompany their stories.

Materials

- *The Talking Eggs* by Robert D. San Souci
- *The Rainbow Fish* by Marcus Pfister
- plain white paper egg
- decorated paper egg
- tin foil scale

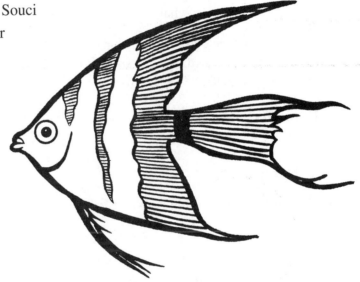

Sample Prop Story Starters

❑ Tell about a time you were walking on the beach and you found a mysterious object stuck in the sand.

❑ Write a story telling how you went about trying to find a lost pet.

❑ Write a story about a time someone got hurt playing a sport.

❑ Write a story about a time you arrived at school without your homework.

❑ Write a story about what happened one night when your mom or dad cooked dinner.

The Mystery of the . . .

Mysteries can be difficult to write, but following this outline should help students on their way to writing a positively enthralling mystery of their own.

Begin by sharing some simple mysteries, perhaps from the Encyclopedia Brown or Cam Jansen series. Complete a story map for each mystery you read. Begin with the conclusion, or solution to the matter, and have the students list the elements of the mystery (i.e., clues) that helped lead the reader to the correct conclusions. (They're always easier to spot after discovering the correct answer!) Have students complete the story map on page 39 backwards, as well. Then they should determine a way to divide their story into five parts for each of the five pages upon which they will write their stories.

Follow the directions below to help students create their story pages. On each following sheet, they should illustrate sneak peeks of what's coming next in their stories.

Following completion of the class' stories, have a "Mystery Party" where students may turn out the lights and share their stories with the class. Before each reader discloses the solution on the last page, the class must guess the outcome of the mystery.

Mystery Booklets

Materials

- activity sheet (page 39)
- 3 sheets of white construction paper for each student
- stapler
- crayons

Directions

Step 1: Measure and fold each sheet of paper at the following distances from the top:

❏ Sheet 1: 2³/₄ inches (7 cm)

❏ Sheet 2: 5¹/₄ inches (13 cm)

❏ Sheet 3: 7³/₄ inches (19 cm)

Step 2: Insert the larger folds into the smaller folds to create a flip book.

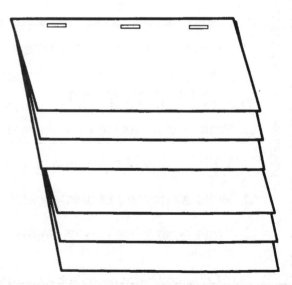

Name _____ Date _____

The Mystery of the . . .

Directions: Mysteries can be a lot of fun to write. Begin by completing this story map backwards. Deciding the outcome of your mystery first can help you plan the plot. Decide what clues you will leave by writing these second. The last thing you will plan is the beginning with the problem or conflict.

Once your map is complete, decide how you can divide your story into five parts, one for each page of your story. The first page will set up the mystery (problem). The second through fourth pages will each hold one clue (plot). The last page will reveal the solution (conflict resolution).

Illustrate the cover of your mystery on the top flap of the booklet. On each flap draw an illustration to give the reader a hint about what happens next in your story. Write the story under each flap.

Mystery Story Outline

Solution (conflict resolution)

Write how the mystery will be solved. _____

_____

_____

_____

Clues (plot)

Write three clues you will give the reader. Be careful to place them in order from last to first.

3. _____

2. _____

1. _____

The Mystery (beginning with characters, setting, and problem)

_____

_____

_____

_____

The Sweetest Story

Nothing motivates young learners like candy! Students can put their sweet tooth talents to work by creating a story that includes the names (and samples) of three candy bars. First, provide a wide range of bars for each group of students. Divide the candy so each group receives three candy bars. (No two groups should have the same combination of candy bars.) Then the groups write a short story that includes the names of their candy bars. They write their stories on poster board so that the candy may be taped securely to their work. Post the students' creations on desktops around the room or on big book displays in the media center. And be sure to have enough snack-sized candy on hand for when students finish their assignment to ensure that the bars meant for their writing assignment actually end up on their posters! (**Caution:** Be aware of students' food allergies before distributing candy.)

Sample Scenarios for "Sweet" Stories

❑ friends going to see a movie

❑ classmates participating in a pep rally or schoolwide sporting event

❑ a sports team at practice or after the game

❑ a trip to the store with Mom and Dad

Materials

- candy bars (three per group)
- poster paper

- tape
- markers

The Annoying Fly

Everyone knows how annoying pesky bugs can be. Here's a chance for students to demonstrate their frustrations in an illustrated story that has a fly buzzing right through the whole thing!

Students follow the directions on page 41 to fold a piece of paper into a four-page booklet; then use yarn to thread a fake fly into the pages so it may "attack" on every page!

Materials

- large sheet of white construction paper
- white yarn
- plastic fly or black construction paper

- activity sheet (page 41)
- glue or tape

Name _____ Date _____

The Annoying Fly

Directions: Flies can be annoying and pesky bugs. Think about a story that involves just such a creature. Use the directions below to fold a large sheet of construction paper. Follow the lines to form your story outline. Your story will be no more than eight pages long, including the cover page. When your story is finished, glue or tape the yarn in between the folds of the booklet, as shown. Tape, tie, or glue your fly to the end of the yarn. As you read your story, buzz the fly through the pages.

Step 1: Hold the paper tall. Fold down, then across, then down again.

Step 2: Open the paper to the first fold. Cut halfway down the horizontal fold.

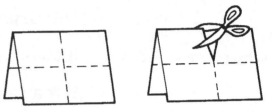

Step 3: Open the paper. Refold so the opening is at the top. Push the two edges together so the cut pages form a square.

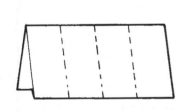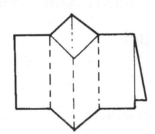

Step 4: Continue pushing to close the gap. Fold all the pages to form an eight-page booklet (including front and back cover).

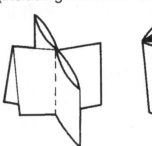

Story Outline

Beginning, including problem or conflict: _____

_____

Events leading up to the conflict resolution: _____

_____

Conclusion: _____

_____

Expository Writing

Yum, Yum!

All About Me

How To...

Futuristic Society

Just for You, Johnny Appleseed!

Three Cheers for the Red, White, and Blue!

Famous People

Meet My Friend

The Ultimate Ice-Cream Sundae

The Graph Club

Body Systems

Country Reports

The Pyramids

Scientifically Speaking

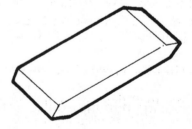

Yum, Yum!

Students will be eager to eat up these creations following this expository writing assignment. List some of the students' favorite foods on the board or on chart paper. Discuss how the students eat these foods: as a meal? on a sandwich? as a snack? Following the directions on page 44, assign students the task of improving their favorite foods by creating an original recipe listing their favorite food as one of the ingredients. Then they write the directions for their new food and draw a picture of the final product. Display the students' creations on an original bulletin board in the cafeteria.

As an extension, students may create a sample of their new food to bring in to share. Brave souls may even wish to have a sampling party!

Materials

- chalkboard or chart paper
- activity sheet (page 44)

All About Me

Who doesn't like to talk about themselves? Students may make use of a multimedia program by creating a presentation describing themselves. Some students may benefit from the outline on page 45 to help organize their ideas and final presentation. As part of their visual enhancer, students can include scanned pictures of themselves involved in the activities they describe.

Students who do not have this kind of technology available to them may wish to complete this activity in typed or written form and secure a picture of themselves to their paper report.

Be sure to allow time each day for students to share their autobiographies. If possible, hook up a television or other presentation monitor to the computer to enlarge the computer screen for the audience.

Variations: The Most Important Thing to Me; The Most Important Person to Me

This activity may be simplified by having students write a report about the most important thing or person to them. They write their essay, then import it into a multimedia report with a scanned photo or digital camera image, or type it and affix their pictures to their reports.

Materials

- multimedia or word-processing software
- activity sheet (page 45)
- personal photos, scanner (if importing photos as a graphic image), or digital camera

Name _____ Date _____

Yum, Yum!

Directions: Think about one of your favorite foods, such as popcorn, chocolate, or hot dogs. List it as the main ingredient.

Now think about how you eat that food. Is it as a snack? a meal? a sandwich? Write a new, original recipe using your favorite food as the main ingredient. Give it a catchy name. List all the ingredients, then explain the directions for making your new food item.

Recipe for _____

Main Ingredient _____

Other Ingredients

❑ _____   ❑ _____

❑ _____   ❑ _____

❑ _____   ❑ _____

❑ _____   ❑ _____

❑ _____   ❑ _____

Directions _____

_____

_____

_____

_____

_____

_____

_____

_____

Name _____ Date _____

All About Me

Directions: Think about three topics to describe yourself. You may choose two or three from the list below or think of some of your own. Then list the features about yourself that fit into the topics you selected. On the back side of this paper, write individual paragraphs for each topic.

Topics

❑ favorite hobbies   ❑ my family

❑ sports I like to play   ❑ what I look like

❑ games I like to play   ❑ my personality

❑ favorite foods   ❑ places I've been

Topic 1: _____

Features or examples: _____

_____

_____

_____

Topic 2: _____

Features or examples: _____

_____

_____

_____

Topic 3: _____

Features or examples: _____

_____

_____

_____

Standards and Benchmarks: 1A, 1B, 1C, 1F, 2A, 2B, 2C

How To...

Who can follow those "simple" directions that accompany most "assemble yourself" contraptions? Oftentimes the writers know what they mean but the readers have a difficult time understanding their directions. The activity sheet on page 47 will help students practice this necessary skill by first having them think of something they are quite good at, such as jumping rope, hammering a nail, or selecting a book from the library. Students then explain to their audience the simple steps to follow, writing each on the following pages of an accordion-folded sheet of drawing paper cut 6" x 18". Folded in 3" increments, this gives the students six 6" x 3" spaces in which to write their directions. They may only write one step in each square, so they must choose an activity that can be completed in less than six steps. Each step is accompanied by a diagram or drawing of their explanation. When the final drafts are complete, have the students trade instruction booklets and try each other's instructions.

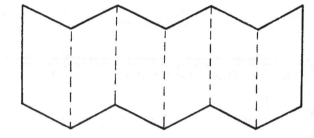

Materials

- activity sheet (page 47)
- drawing paper cut into 6" x 18" pieces

Standards and Benchmarks: 1A, 1B, 1C, 1E, 1F, 1G

Futuristic Society

How do students of today envision life of tomorrow? This three-dimensional art and corresponding writing activity will have them ready for their futures. Give each team of students a shoe box in which to create their vision of the future. They may create a diorama of a city, house, school, invention, or any other futuristic dream. After constructing their visual, they will write an expository essay describing their model. The student activity on page 48 may help students organize their thoughts and plan their models and essays. The teams should then decide how to attach their essays to their dioramas. Display the results in the media center or on a display table in the classroom.

Materials

- miscellaneous art supplies with which to construct a diorama of the future
- shoe box for each team of students
- activity sheet (page 48)

Innovation on a good idea

In place of dioramas, students may prefer to create a hanging mobile of their ideas. Provide the necessary materials, and suspend the students' work from the ceiling. Instead of attaching their report to their mobile, they may orally share their work and refer to the mobile as a visual aid.

How To...

Directions: Think about an activity that you are good at, such as jumping rope, hammering a nail, or selecting a book from the library. You should be able to write the directions to your activity in six or fewer steps.

Now think about how you would explain to someone else how to do this same activity. Write your six or fewer steps on the lines below.

Use a sheet of drawing paper cut 6" by 18". Accordion fold the paper into six 3" sections. Write each step of your activity in a section. Include a diagram or drawing for each step.

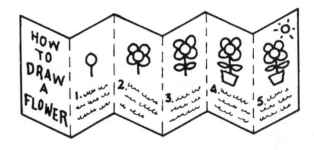

How to _____

Step 1 _____

_____

Step 2 _____

_____

Step 3 _____

_____

Step 4 _____

_____

Step 5 _____

_____

Step 6 _____

_____

Futuristic Society

Directions: Think about what life in the future will be like. You may wish to describe life in general, or select one aspect of the future (such as transportation, communications, or clothing) to describe. In the box below, create a visual image. Then, on the lines beneath your drawing, explain how life in the future will be different from life today. Use additional pages as needed.

_____

_____

_____

_____

_____

Just for You, Johnny Appleseed!

Following a study of this historic figure, ask the students to brainstorm ways his job might have been made easier with the help of more modern conveniences. In teams or pairs, have the students design and create an actual model of a device that might have helped Johnny Appleseed distribute seeds throughout his journeys. Students may use simple arts and crafts supplies such as cotton, craft sticks, strawberry containers, yarn, construction paper, paper plates, or pipe cleaners to construct their models. Then they create a poster (see student activity page 50) to name their contraption, label its parts, and explain how it works. Allow time for the teams to share their "machines," then display them in the library or elsewhere in the school for all to enjoy.

Materials

- miscellaneous art supplies
- activity sheet (page 50)

Three Cheers for the Red, White and Blue!

People show their patriotism in many ways. Some attend parades, fly flags, give donations to veteran societies, or visit memorials to honor our nation's past. Brainstorm as a class the various ways people show their patriotism. Then the students use the activity sheet on page 51 to show their true colors by writing an essay explaining how they may show their patriotism. Of course, this assignment wouldn't be complete without a little color! Students mount their essays onto red, white, or blue construction paper and create patriotic collages to border their works. Proudly display these patriotic works of art on a bulletin board or in a hallway so everyone may appreciate the class' work.

Materials

- activity sheet (page 51)
- red construction paper
- white construction paper
- blue construction paper
- glue

Innovations on a good idea

Another option is to have students word process their essay, then print it on patriotic printing paper. Or they may import a decorative border from a clip art program, or design and create their own border by using the drawing application of their favorite word-processing program and print a colored border right along with their essay.

Just for You, Johnny Appleseed!

Directions: Johnny Appleseed spent his life walking from place to place distributing seeds in little sacks. Think about a device Johnny Appleseed could have used to help him distribute seeds more easily. In the box below, draw your invention. Then label its parts and, on the lines below your drawing, explain how the device works. Use additional pages, if needed.

_____

_____

_____

_____

_____

Name _____   Date _____

Three Cheers for the Red, White, and Blue!

Directions: People show their patriotism in many ways, such as attending parades; flying flags; giving donations; or wearing red, white, and blue. Think about two or three ways people can show their patriotism. Use the lines below to explain how people exhibit their patriotism. Mount your paper onto a slightly larger sheet of construction paper; then use red, white, and blue scraps to create a patriotic collage around your essay.

_____

_____

_____

_____

_____

_____

_____

_____

_____

_____

_____

_____

_____

_____

_____

Standards and Benchmarks: 1A, 1B, 1C, 1F, 1G, 4B, 4G

Famous People

When completing their next famous-person report, students can use this visual accompaniment to jazz up what might otherwise seem to be a dull presentation. After students complete their reports, give them the supplies listed below and allow them to create masks of their famous people. When sharing their reports with the class, students don their masks so the class has the chance to "meet" the famous person.

Materials

- research materials
- outline sheet (page 53)
- paper plate and craft stick
- yarn, construction paper, markers, etc.
- glue
- scissors

Innovations on a good idea

Students may complete this same activity when writing an essay to explain how a person's character traits played a key role in determining his or her actions in a story. When students read their reports to the class, they may wear masks of the characters they are discussing. For example, students writing about the story "Ben and Me" may wish to explain how Amos' personality traits affected his actions in the story, or they may wish to give examples of how Ben's personality contributed to his actions. The students would then make masks of Amos or Ben and use these masks as props when giving their reports to the class.

Standards and Benchmarks: 1A, 1B, 1C, 1F, 1G, 2A

Meet My Friend

Students follow the directions on page 54 to share the reasons why their friend is their best friend. Then they use drawing paper to draw a portrait of their friend to include on a bulletin board entitled "Meet My Friend."

Materials

- activity sheet (page 54)
- 9" by 12" (23 cm by 30 cm) sheet of drawing paper
- paints, markers, or crayons

Innovations on a good idea

If completing this assignment electronically with the help of a multimedia program, students may wish to include scanned or digital-camera images of their best friends in their reports. Attach an overhead projector or large screen monitor to your computer to allow the students to share their friends with the class in bright, bold color!

Name _____ Date _____

Famous Person Report

Directions: Use research materials to gather information about a famous person. Answer the questions below. Then use this information to help guide a report about your famous person.

Famous Person _____

Personal Information

	Born	Died
Date		
Place		

Childhood _____

_____

_____

Education _____

_____

_____

Professional Information

Why is this person famous? _____

_____

_____

_____

How has his or her fame affected society? _____

_____

_____

Additional Information

Other interesting facts and information about this person: _____

_____

_____

Name _____ Date _____

Meet My Friend

Directions: Everyone has a best friend who is unlike anyone else. Think about your best friend and his or her best qualities, such as she makes you laugh or he listens to your problems. Write an essay to explain why this person is your best friend. Be sure to include examples and details to describe this person's personality. For example, tell about a time she made you laugh or he listened to a problem you were having and any solution he offered.

Use the back of this page or a separate sheet of drawing paper to draw a portrait of your best friend.

My Best Friend

_____

_____

_____

_____

_____

_____

_____

_____

_____

_____

_____

_____

_____

_____

_____

_____

_____

_____

Standards and Benchmarks: 1A, 1F, 2A

The Ultimate Ice-Cream Sundae

Everyone has his or her own favorite sundae toppings (not to mention ice-cream flavors upon which to build his or her creation). Students can practice their "how to" essays by explaining to their audience how they would build their own ultimate ice cream sundae.

Materials

- activity sheet (page 56)
- crayons

Standards and Benchmarks: 1A, 1B, 1C, 1F, 1G, 2A, 4F, 4G

The Graph Club

Graphs and charts can add to any informational essay that includes surveys, data, or other numerical comparisons. Students may practice with the activity on page 57, then try any of the following situations independently to include graphs and charts in their works. (The following data may be collected, then changed from a bar graph to a pie chart by figuring the percent of each figure.) Encourage students to share their findings. They may enlarge the graph to use as a visual during a mock television report or place the information on an overhead to use when sharing their findings with the class.

Materials

- activity sheet (page 57)
- chart or poster paper (optional)
- graphing software (optional)
- overhead transparencies (optional)

Sample graphing and chart-making assignments

- ❑ number of classmates who like different sports
- ❑ number of students who have birthdays in different months
- ❑ number of students wearing laces, buckles, Velcro, or slip-on shoes
- ❑ number of minutes each student spends on homework each week
- ❑ number of siblings in each student's family
- ❑ number of each color of the chocolate-coated candies in a bag

---

Name _____   Date _____

The Ultimate Ice-Cream Sundae

Directions: Have you ever wanted the chance to create your own ice cream sundae? Well, this assignment will have you drooling for this frozen treat! First think about the ice cream flavor(s) that would act as the foundation for your treat, and determine how many scoops of each flavor you will need. Then drown the ice cream with any and all toppings you can think of.

Now that you have a visual image of your sundae, explain to someone how to go about creating it. Use the template below. Begin your directions in the ice cream dish at the bottom. Add paragraphs up the sundae and finish at the top. Color your creation and decorate it as best you can without covering up your words.

Name _____ Date _____

The Graph Club

Directions: Graphs and charts can add to any assignment that requires an explanation of numerical data. Collect the data you need. Create a bar graph and then write a report explaining what the data shows, how it was collected, and what conclusions you can draw from the results.

Assignment: Survey your classmates to determine how many pencils they have in their desks.

Number of Pencils

Students

This data shows _____

_____

_____

_____

_____

I gathered this data by _____

_____

_____

_____

Based on the data, I conclude that _____

_____

_____

_____

Standards and Benchmarks: 1A, 1B, 1C, 1E, 1F, 1G, 2A, 4F, 4G

Body Systems

This very complicated unit of study can be simplified through the use of visual aides. Students select (or are assigned) a body system topic (e.g., respiratory, skeletal, muscular, internal) to research and study. They then complete a colored model of their system on the graphic on page 59 and write a detailed description explaining how that system works and the role it plays in the daily functions of the human body. Another option is to allow students to trace their own bodies on large paper and diagram their system on a life-size model. Post the students' work in the hallway or around the room.

Materials

- activity sheet (page 59)
- research materials

Standards and Benchmarks: 1A, 1B, 1C, 1E, 1F, 2A, 4F, 4G

Country Reports

Explaining about a country is never quite as impressive as a personal visit. Failing this, pictures and memorabilia may do just as well to enhance a country report. Students use their research skills and the organizational graphics on pages 60–64 to write a comprehensive report about a country of their choosing (or one that has been assigned to them). Each component of the report may then be secured to a large sheet of poster paper for a simplified visual display. Or students may wish to create an individual booklet of their report by securing the pages inside the fold of a large sheet of construction paper. They may then decorate the outside of the booklet with enticing graphics and a title.

Materials

- Country Report: Geography (page 60)
- Country Report: Production (page 61)
- Country Report: Cuisine (page 62)
- Country Report: Clothing (page 63)
- Country Report: Architecture (page 64)

- reference sources
- activity sheets
- poster paper (optional)
- large sheet of construction paper (optional)

Innovation on a good idea

Instead of a written report, students may create an interactive tour of their assigned country with the use of a multimedia program. They may include scanned photos or they may download pictures from the Internet to include in their electronic tour. Allow time for two or three groups each day to take the class on a virtual field trip of their destination. After all the countries have been shown, have the class vote on the location they would most like to visit. Discuss how the report enticed them to choose this location.

Name _____ Date _____

Body Systems

Directions: Use colored pencils or crayons to illustrate the active body system you are studying. For example, draw all the major muscles and the directions they move. Then explain how the body system works and why it is important.

This is the

_____

System

How this body system works:

_____

_____

_____

_____

_____

_____

This body system is important because _____

_____

_____

_____

_____ .

Name _____   Date _____

Country Report: Geography

Directions: Research the geography of the country you are studying. Draw a map of the country, including the surrounding areas and major bodies of water, mountain ranges, or other important geographical features. Then explain the map on the lines below.

My Country

_____

Continent

_____

Capital City

_____

Population

_____

Explain the geography of your country.

_____

_____

_____

_____

_____

Country Report: Production

Directions: Research the agricultural and industrial products that come from the country you are studying. Draw a map showing where these products can be found, or draw the items that your country is most famous for.

My Country

_____

Agricultural Products

_____

_____

_____

Industrial Products

_____

_____

_____

Explain the agricultural and industrial products found in your country.

_____

_____

_____

_____

_____

_____

Name _____   Date _____

Country Report: Cuisine

Directions: Research some traditional foods that people from the country you are studying enjoy. Draw them on the plates. Include some customary drinks, if you can. Then explain the local cuisine on the lines below.

My Country _____

Explain the cuisine of your country.

_____

_____

_____

Country Report: Clothing

Directions: Research some traditional clothing that people from the country you are studying wear. Dress the boy and girl paper dolls to represent this country's native dress. Then explain the clothing on the lines below.

My Country _____

Explain the clothing worn in your country.

_____

_____

_____

Name _____ Date _____

Country Report: Architecture

Directions: Discover one or two important or famous buildings, structures, or landmarks that are famous tourist attractions in the country you are studying. Draw what the front of a postcard from your country might look like in the top box. Use the lines below the drawing to explain the history or significance of the place(s) you have illustrated on your postcard.

My Country _____

_____

_____

_____

_____

_____

_____

The Pyramids

Egyptians spent a great deal of time planning, building, and preparing their pyramids. What students learn about these wonders of the world may be explained on the sides of a model pyramid.

Materials

- activity sheet (page 66)
- scissors
- tape

Scientifically Speaking

Verbalizing orally or in written form the process and outcome of a favorite experiment is an authentic way of helping students internalize and take ownership of their learning. Following a unit of study, as a class, brainstorm a list of experiments the students performed. While creating their lists, students verbalize the process of carrying out the experiment and the outcomes or conclusions they drew from their findings. Students then select their favorite experiment and explain the entire process from start to finish. The outline on page 67 may help students further organize their ideas. Included, also, is a visual to help the students' explanations. The visual might take the form of a graph of the data or a drawing of a part of the experiment.

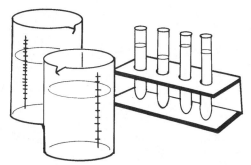

Materials

- activity sheet (page 67)

Innovation on a good idea

Have the students write to explain their favorite experiment in a letter to the principal. Since they weren't part of the original experimentation, the students will really have to think to explain the process and outcomes as if the principal wished to re-create the experiment himself or herself.

The Pyramids

Directions: Write what you learned about the pyramids on this model of a pyramid. Explain the topics on each side. Cut out the model and fold on the dotted lines. Tape the edges together to form a pyramid.

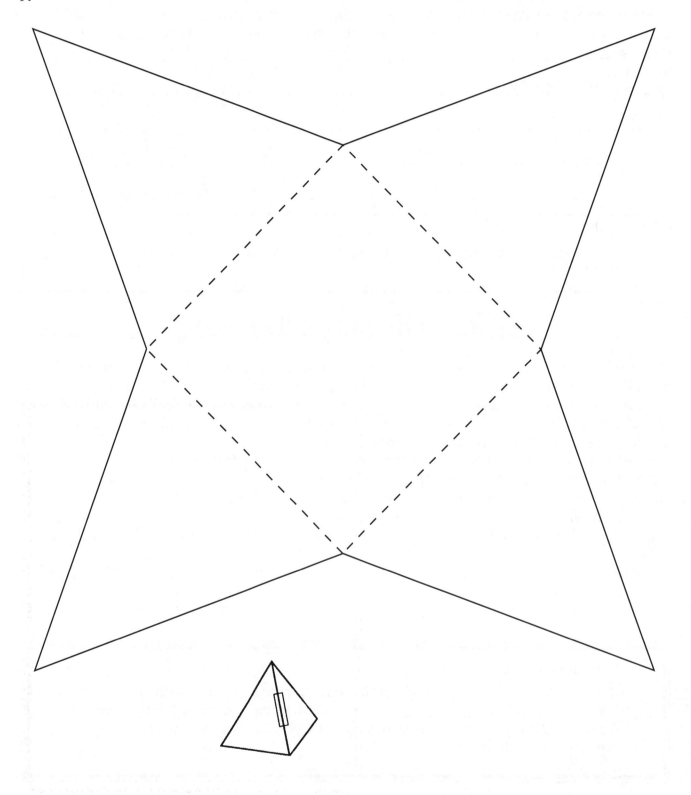

Name _____ Date _____

Scientifically Speaking

Directions: Think about a particularly interesting science experiment you've conducted. Every experiment has a purpose, procedures, and a conclusion based upon the data. Explain your favorite experiment from start to finish. Then include a graph of the data you collected, or draw a picture of the procedures or conclusion to help explain what you did.

Science Topic _____

Purpose of the Experiment _____

_____

_____

_____

What We Did (Procedures) _____

_____

_____

_____

What It Looked Like

Our Findings (Conclusion) _____

_____

_____

_____

_____

_____

_____

_____

Persuasive Writing

On the Playground

Futuristic Fun Time

Current Events

The Best Thanksgiving Dinner Ever

The Reluctant Leprechaun

Persuasive Advertising

But, Mom!!!

Dear Mr. President

Healthy Eating, Healthy Day

Keys to Good Test Taking

A Good Book, Anyone?

Nursery Rhyme Time

Learn to Conserve!

From the Ground Up

Stadium Proposal

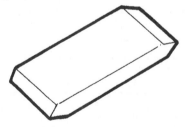

On the Playground

A new item of playground equipment (or a replacement of some old apparatus) can certainly get students motivated to come to school. But what if they were actually part of the decision-making process when the time came to decide what to buy?

First, take a tour of the playground and have students create a map of the equipment that already exists. Back in class, ask your students to think about the playground equipment that's already on the playground, rank it in order from best to worst (you can also make a graph of the students' favorites), and consider what may be missing from their playground or what might need to be replaced with a new and improved model. Then they use what they know about the most popular equipment at their school and compare it with other equipment they've seen at the park or other location to decide what they think they would buy if their school had $5,000 to spend on new playground equipment. You may wish to supply students with some recent equipment catalogs so they may make even more informed decisions to persuade the administration as to which apparatus to buy.

After the students have completed their letters, invite the students to read their persuasive letters to the class. The class decides on the most persuasive letters and tells why they were so effective. Then the two top persuaders debate their ideas orally for the class. Conduct a class vote. Which piece of equipment do they now think is the best choice?

Materials:

- activity sheets (pages 70 and 71)
- equipment catalogs

Futuristic Fun Time

Have you ever thought about what toys of the future might look like? Students play the role of inventor by selecting a toy or game of today from a magazine, then writing to persuade the makers of the product to make it more modern or hi-tech for the future.

Materials

- toy catalogs or magazines with toy advertisements
- activity sheet (page 72)
- glue
- scissors

Name _____   Date _____

On the Playground

Directions: What new equipment would you buy if you had $5,000 to spend on your school's playground? Your job is to think about the equipment that already exists on your playground and write a letter persuading your principal what to buy. Perhaps you have some new equipment in mind, or perhaps you would like to see an old piece of equipment replaced.

In either case, your first task is to make a map of the playground. Use symbols to show the locations of the equipment. Make a map key. Then think about the new equipment you wish to buy and where it would go. Include this in your map. Then write a letter to your principal explaining why this equipment is the best choice to buy.

Playground Map   **Map Key**

On the Playground *(cont.)*

Directions: Your school has just been awarded $5,000 with which to buy some new playground equipment. Write a letter to your principal explaining why the equipment you want is the best purchase he or she can make with the money.

Date _____

Dear _____,

I am excited about our school receiving some new playground equipment. I think the best way to spend the $5,000 is to buy _____

because _____

_____

_____

_____

_____

_____

_____

_____

Sincerely,

_____

Name _____   Date _____

Futuristic Fun Time

Directions: Here's your chance to persuade a toy manufacturer to modernize their wares. Look through some toy catalogs or magazines with toy advertisements. Or, simply think about a toy you think could be so much better if only it were computerized and draw a picture of it. Then write a letter to the maker of the toy persuading them why they should modernize this toy.

Date _____

Dear _____,

I have been thinking about one of your toys and how it might be improved for the 21st century. The toy is _____. I think you should change it by

_____

_____

_____

_____

_____

_____

Sincerely,

_____

Standards and Benchmarks: 1A, 1B, 1C, 1E, 1F, 1J, 1K, 2B, 4G

Current Events

Students can speak their minds and express their thoughts by first reading about a controversial event happening in the world today, then writing an editorial to support or condemn a new policy or a person's actions. *Time for Kids* and *Cobblestone Magazine* make great sources to get students interested in what's going on in the present and past. Also check your local newspaper for appropriate articles on topics in which you think your students might show an interest. For example, students might read a newspaper article about a recent oil spill and the effects it has had on the environment. Depending on the circumstances surrounding the accident and the information shared in the article, students may respond to the question, "Should the government enforce higher safety laws regarding oil rigs. If so, what should they be? If not, explain why you think the current laws are sufficient."

In addition to writing a persuasive essay in response to the article they've read, students create a rally poster to express their side of the issue. Post the students' work on a bulletin board or in the hallway to demonstrate the two sides of the issue.

Materials

- news article or other nonfiction passage about a current or past issue
- activity sheet (page 74)
- poster paper or large construction paper

Standards and Benchmarks: 1A, 1C, 1E, 1F, 1J, 2A

The Best Thanksgiving Dinner Ever

Some people's best memories are of Thanksgiving dinner at Grandma's. Regardless of where your students spend their Thanksgiving holiday, they probably think their chef's cooking is the best. Students use their own hand outline to create a turkey, then write sentences in each finger to persuade others that their meal is the best. Have the students cut out their turkeys and use them as part of a holiday bulletin board.

Materials

- activity sheet (page 75)
- scissors

Name _____   Date _____

Current Events

Directions: Read an article about a recent or past event that encourages disagreement over an issue. Write a one- or two-sentence summary. Think about the two sides of the story and decide with whom you agree. Write a paragraph to try to persuade others to agree with your viewpoint. If writing an essay, use additional paper, if needed. On the back of this page, design a poster to visually explain your opinion.

Title of Article _____

Summary _____

_____

_____

Two Sides of the Story

Side 1	Side 2

What I Think

_____

_____

_____

_____

_____

_____

Name _____   Date _____

The Best Thanksgiving Dinner Ever

Directions: Most people can't imagine being anywhere else for Thanksgiving than where they usually go. Think about where you spend your Thanksgiving holiday and the luscious foods you enjoy. Try to persuade a classmate that your grandma, mom, aunt, dad, or cousin is the BEST Thanksgiving cook around.

Place your hand flat against the bottom of this page, then trace around it. Use your hand outline to draw a turkey. Use your thumb as the turkey's head. Then write four sentences explaining why your Thanksgiving feast is the best, one sentence in each finger.

The Reluctant Leprechaun

Students are familiar with Irish folklore that states that if you can catch a leprechaun, you can make him show you where he's hidden his pot of gold. This St. Patrick's Day is your students' lucky day! Students pretend they've caught their quarry, but the leprechaun won't cooperate until the students have written an essay explaining why he should relinquish his riches to them. Students must write a persuasive paper explaining why they should have the pot of gold. After you've read and graded them, attach a shiny, gold-wrapped, chocolate candy at the end of the rainbow to show the students that their paper adequately persuaded you to "share your riches." Display these persuasive works of art on a bulletin board entitled "Lucky Pot of Gold."

Materials

- activity sheet (page 77)
- gold-wrapped chocolate candies
- tape

Persuasive Advertising

An advertisement's purpose is to persuade the consumer to purchase the company's product. Some advertising ploys are more effective than others. As a class, describe some commercials, billboards, and magazine ads the students have seen; or ask students to clip some interesting ones ahead of time to bring to class to discuss. Have the students analyze the campaign to determine how the manufacturers get the consumers' interest and ultimately (they hope) entice consumers to buy their product.

Next have the students hunt through their desks to find something for which they will develop an advertisement. They may select their favorite pencil, pen, pencil box, or maybe even a math book! Students use the activity sheet on page 78 to plan and develop their advertisement. They may wish to create a poster, billboard, or electronic "commercial" to promote the product they have chosen. Allow time in class for students to share their advertisements. Discuss with the class which was the most persuasive and why.

Materials

- activity sheet (page 78)
- advertisement clippings (optional)
- poster paper
- multimedia software

The Reluctant Leprechaun

Directions: Leprechauns are supposed to show you where they've hidden their pot of gold—if you can ever catch one. But what if you did and he refused? How would you persuade a leprechaun to take you to his pot of gold? Think of some ideas explaining to this uncooperative leprechaun why you deserve the pot of gold. Write a sentence in each band of the rainbow.

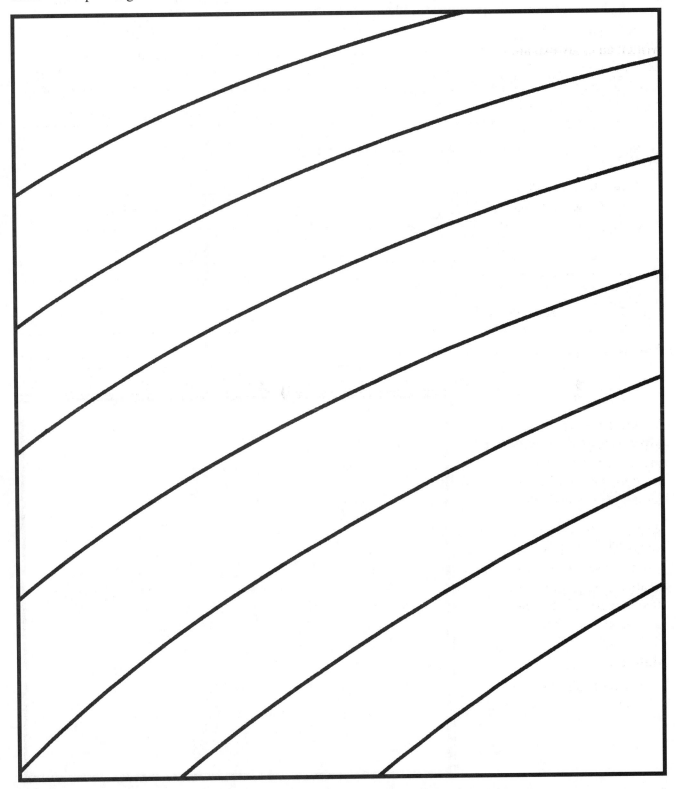

Name _____ Date _____

Persuasive Advertising

Directions: Advertisers work very hard to persuade consumers to buy their products. Look in your desk and select an item for which to write an advertisement. You may choose a favorite pencil, pen, pencil box, or maybe even a math book! Think about how you would advertise the product you chose. Organize your thoughts below. Then create a poster, billboard, or electronic "commercial" using a multimedia program to advertise your product.

Item: _____

Interesting or unique features: _____

_____

Three reasons why someone should own this product

1. _____

   _____

2. _____

   _____

3. _____

   _____

Advertising Plan (circle one)

❏ Poster

❏ Billboard

❏ Commercial

❏ Other _____

But, Mom!!!

Sometimes parents' decisions seem unfair, but usually they act in their children's best interest. How do the students in your class try to persuade their parents to bend to their wishes? Lead a class discussion about some ploys in which the students engage, and ask students to cite specific examples of when they've been successful. Then encourage students to think of times when their parents simply wouldn't give in to their wishes; ask them to share these experiences. Encourage the students to share the debates in which they engaged with their parents to try to persuade them to change their minds.

Based on their experiences, which of the two scenarios happens more often? Why do they think that is? Explain that with this activity, students will get the chance to anticipate what their parents will say when they ask to do something to which they think their parents won't agree. Students will then have the opportunity to plan counterpoints related to their parents' arguments.

Following completion of the project, have the students role play the two sides of the issue. Ask two volunteers to be the parents and one person to be the child. Who do the students think will win the debate? Why?

Materials

- activity sheet (page 80)

Dear Mr. President

Following a study of American civil rights and the suffrage movement, have the students take on the role of either of these groups as they attempt to persuade the president of the era to take action on their behalf. Their letters should persuade the president to see their side of the inequalities and explain what action they wish him to take, based on historical fact. Students should use the information they learned from the unit to appropriately date and address their letters as well as raise issues evident during that era.

To enhance their letter visually, students create an original slogan and graphic to represent their opinions of the subject matter. If possible, share some common equal rights visuals, such as the dove or two shaking hands.

Materials

- activity sheet (page 81)
- Civil Rights symbols

But, Mom!!!

Directions: Your best friend has just invited you to go with his or her family on a trip to Disney World. Normally, this wouldn't be a problem: your parents would love for you to go. But the vacation takes place over the holidays. You know your mom and dad aren't going to let you go unless you can persuade them otherwise. Think about how you will try to persuade your parents to let you take a trip with a friend over the holidays. Plan your key points below to use when you ask your parents if you can go.

Point

Why my parents will say "no"

Counterpoint

Why I should be able to go

1 _____   ➡   1 _____
_____   _____
_____   _____
_____   _____
_____   _____

2 _____   ➡   2 _____
_____   _____
_____   _____
_____   _____
_____   _____

3 _____   ➡   3 _____
_____   _____
_____   _____
_____   _____
_____   _____

Name _____ Date _____

Dear Mr. President

Directions: Think about the message you would want to send to the President of the United States regarding your civil rights as a minority living during the 1960s or a woman living from 1890 to 1920. Write a letter to persuade him to take action on your behalf. To visually enhance your position, create an original slogan and graphic to represent your point on the subject matter. Use the back side of this page.

_____

Dear Mr. President:

I feel very strongly that I am entitled to the same civil rights as _____

_____

_____

_____

_____

_____

_____

_____

Thank you for taking the time to consider my position on this matter.

Sincerely,

_____

Healthy Eating, Healthy Day

Following a study of the food pyramid, students can use this visual to persuade others to eat healthy meals for at least one day. Using the serving recommendations as a guide, they develop a meal plan for one day in a three-part pyramid, each section representing breakfast, lunch, or dinner. Challenge the students to follow their meal plan for one day and discuss the difficulties they had in sticking to the plan.

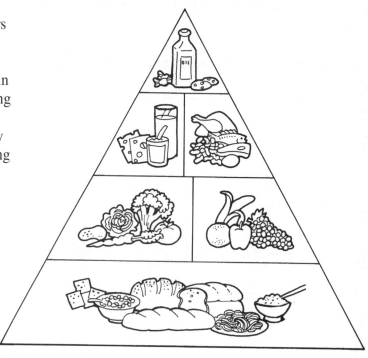

Materials

- copy of the food pyramid, if needed
- activity sheet (page 83)

Standards and Benchmarks: 1A, 4F

Keys To Good Test Taking

Most students are required to take some formal assessment at least once during their elementary-school careers. Having practiced for the test is only half the battle. Students can achieve better test scores by preparing the evening before and the day of the test. Lead a discussion about the ways students prepare themselves for regular tests in class, such as for math or science. Besides studying the content, ask them to think of additional tips they can follow to be prepared on test day (e.g., eating a healthy breakfast, getting a good night's rest, etc.). After starting a list of three or four items, have the students continue to think independently and complete the activity sheet on page 84.

Following their brainstorming session, the students may create posters of their ideas to post in the hallways to encourage test preparedness throughout the school.

Materials

- activity sheet (page 84)
- colored paper
- construction paper
- glue
- scissors

Name _____ Date _____

Healthy Eating, Healthy Day

Directions: Eating healthy foods and trying to stick to the recommended daily allowances are habits everyone should try to follow. Use the food pyramid to plan three healthy meals; record your healthful meals within the divisions of the template below. Remember to count the numbers of servings in the food groups for the day to make sure you have included enough of the correct kinds of foods.

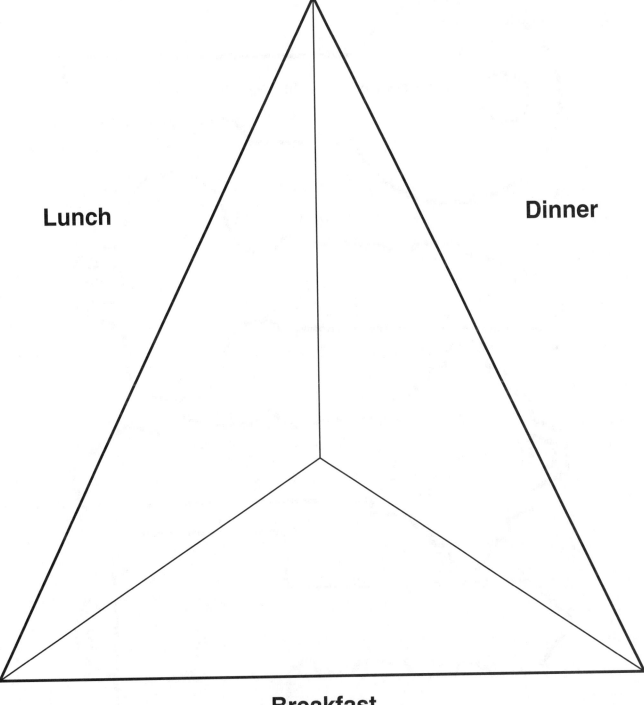

Lunch

Dinner

Breakfast

Keys to Good Test Taking

Directions: Listening in class, taking good notes, and studying are just some ways people prepare for a test. Think about additional advice you might give a classmate to help get ready for a test you have tomorrow. Write three "keys" to good test taking in the key shapes below.

Eat a healthy breakfast, like eggs, toast, and juice.

A Good Book, Anyone?

Take your typical book report assignment and turn it into a persuasive task that's sure to leave students ready to read more, more, more! Students use the mask outline on page 87 to create a "Mardi Gras"-style mask to wear when attempting to persuade their classmates to read a book they've read. For added durability, use the mask outline as a template to trace onto a plain white paper plate, then attach a craft stick to one side so students may hold onto their masks while giving their reports. Post the students' persuasive essays along with their masks on a bulletin board so students may refer to it when deciding on their next library selection.

Materials

- activity sheet (page 86)
- mask outline (page 87)
- yarn
- hole punch
- miscellaneous art supplies (e.g., feathers, cotton, construction paper, etc.)
- plain white paper plates (optional)
- craft sticks (optional)

Innovations on a good idea

Students may wish to persuade their classmates to read a book by completing any of the following alternative assignments. Each activity requires different materials, depending on the involvement and creativity of the students. They may still complete the persuasive book report outline provided on page 86.

- ❏ setting, character, or plot mobile
- ❏ commercial to advertise the story
- ❏ setting, character, or plot diorama
- ❏ movie action poster
- ❏ character puppets

- ❏ trivia game show
- ❏ reader's theater
- ❏ bookmark advertisement
- ❏ multimedia report
- ❏ television interview with the main character

Name _____ Date _____

A Good Book, Anyone?

Directions: Reading a good book is like making a new friend. Sharing this treasure with your classmates and persuading them to read it, too, is like giving a very special gift. Use the book report outline below to persuade your classmates to read a book you've read. Then create a mask, poster, commercial or other visual to accompany the report you've written.

Title _____

Author _____ Illustrator_____

Copyright Information _____

The characters in this book were the most fascinating you'll ever meet in a story. One of them, in particular, was especially memorable.

_____

_____

_____

The main character's task was to _____

_____

_____.

Lots of _____ events happened along the way. For
(strange, funny, exciting, etc.)

example, _____

_____

_____.

But the best part was when _____

_____

_____

_____.

A Good Book, Anyone? *(cont.)*

Use this mask outline with "A Good Book, Anyone?" Have the students use art supplies to decorate the mask like one of the characters in their story. Punch holes on either side of the mask and attach yarn for the students to tie around the backs of their heads before giving their book reports.

Standards and Benchmarks: 1E, 1F, 1H, 1L

Nursery Rhyme Time

What would have happened if Jack and Jill's parents had told them to be more careful when fetching that pail of water? or if Jack had met a peddler selling magic eggs before he'd met the man with the magic beans? or if Mary could verbally persuade her lamb to stay where it was supposed to?

Students take this opportunity to think about a favorite nursery rhyme, then create a persuasive dialogue between two people in the rhyme that would affect its outcome. A picture accompanies their dialogue to show the new end result.

Materials

- activity sheet (page 89)
- crayons

Suggested nursery rhyme situations

❑ Little Miss Muffet's best friend invites her to sit with her to eat her whey.

❑ A child convinces the itsy bitsy spider to build a web under a window sill.

❑ Mary persuades a friend to lamb-sit while she is in school.

❑ The King's horses and the King's men suggest another activity for Humpty Dumpty.

❑ Jill implores Jack to fetch water from a well in town instead of on a steep hill.

Standards and Benchmarks: 1A, 1F, 1J, 1K, 4F

Learn to Conserve

The world's depleted energy resources and abundance of garbage are cause for concern in the future (and even the present) if we don't start taking the proper steps to right some obvious wrongs. If possible, share some recent articles related to this topic with your students from your local newspaper or other student-directed periodical. As a class, brainstorm a list of ways people might conserve the resources available to us on Earth. Students then work in pairs, independently, or in groups to complete the flow chart on page 90 meant to persuade others to consider the future when next they throw away recyclable materials, waste water, or overuse electrical appliances. Encourage students to then transfer their flow charts to poster paper and display them in the hallway or local supermarket for everyone to see.

Materials

- article related to energy or resource conservation
- activity sheet (page 90)
- poster paper (optional)

Name _____ Date _____

Nursery Rhyme Time

Directions: Think about one of your favorite nursery rhymes, such as "Jack and Jill" or "Mary Had a Little Lamb." Knowing how the tale ends, write a dialogue between two characters where one is trying to persuade the other to change his or her ways. For example, Mary might try to persuade a friend to "lamb-sit" for her so she could go to school and not get into trouble; or Jill might persuade Jack to fetch water from the well in town instead of on the hill where he might get hurt. Following your dialogue, draw a picture on the back side of this page to show the new outcome of the nursery rhyme.

Nursery Rhyme: _____

Character	Dialogue

Learn to Conserve!

Directions: Think about an energy or natural resource and how people might reduce, reuse, or recycle this resource and why. Use the flow chart below to demonstrate what might happen if this resource continues to be depleted and what might happen if it's conserved.

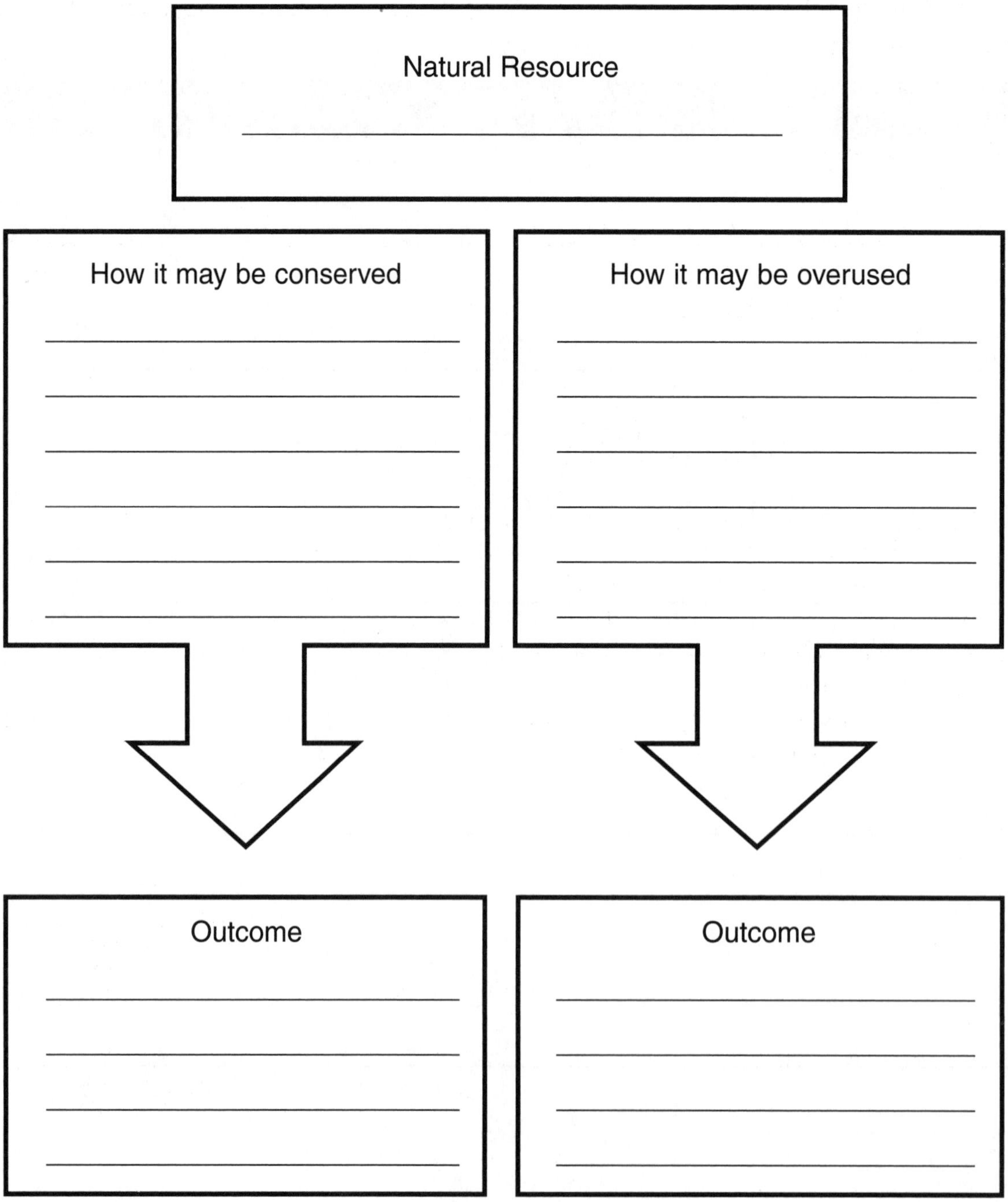

Natural Resource

_____

How it may be conserved

_____
_____
_____
_____
_____
_____

How it may be overused

_____
_____
_____
_____
_____
_____

Outcome

_____
_____
_____
_____

Outcome

_____
_____
_____
_____

From the Ground Up

Students studying Colonial times and the layout of the various towns may try their hand at organizing a new town's buildings by first persuading their fellow townspeople to follow their advice as to where to build each structure. Students use the map symbols supplied on the student activity page to map out what they feel is an appropriate location for each building. Then they write persuasive essays detailing their plans to present at the next town meeting. Post the students' work on a bulletin board entitled "The New Colonial America."

Materials

• activity sheet (page 92)

Standards and Benchmarks: 1A, 1B, 1C, 1F, 1G

Stadium Proposal

A lot of planning and development go into the building of a new sports stadium. Students complete the charts on page 93, then use their figures to create an outline of a new stadium on page 94. Decisions as to where each kind of seat should go are then explained in a rationale prepared for their CEO. Following their writing assignment, have the students use miscellaneous art supplies to create a model of their stadium. They transfer their data to an overhead or large chart, then share their findings, diagram, and model with the class. The class acts as if they are the board members considering the student's proposal. Following all the students' presentations, have the class discuss which proposals were more convincing and why.

Materials

• activity sheets (pages 93 and 94)
• writing paper
• miscellaneous art supplies
• glue
• scissors
• blank overheads or chart paper

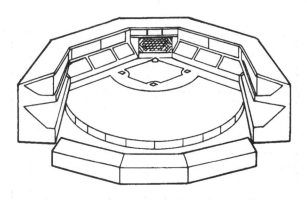

Name _____   Date _____

From the Ground Up

Directions: Colonial towns mostly followed a similar pattern when the buildings were constructed. Think about how you would place each essential building in a new Colonial town. Look at the map below. Use the map key to organize your town. Then give it a name and tell which colony it is in. On the back of this paper, write an explanation (to present at the next town meeting) as to why you placed the buildings where you did .

Colonial Map of

_____

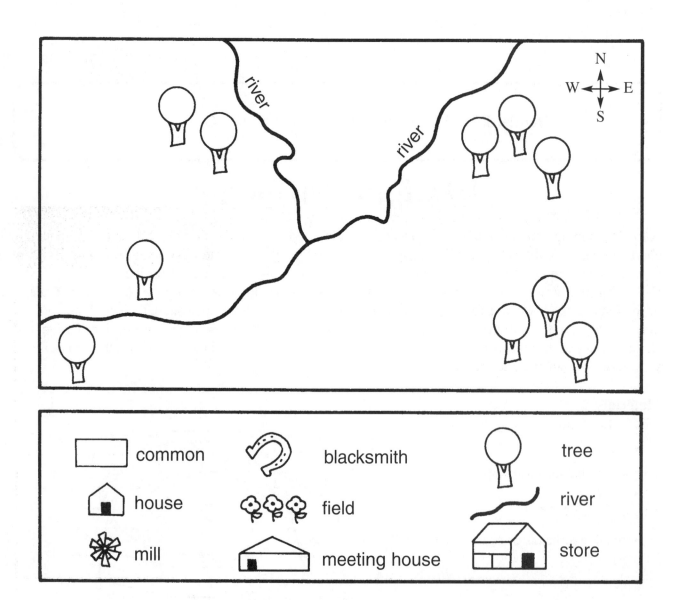

Stadium Proposal

Directions: You are in charge of designing a new sports stadium. Your first task is to determine how many of each seat you wish to include. Complete the chart below, trying different figures in each column. Then assign seating sections on the next page. On the back of the stadium outline, write a rationale for the section assignments. For example, you might explain why you decided section "A" should be the smallest section and section "C" should be the largest section.

Rules of the Game

❏ Each section must have a minimum of 5,000 seats and a maximum of 20,000 seats.

❏ The total number of seats must equal 50,000.

❏ Multiply the number of seats by the cost of each seat to determine the maximum profit for each section.

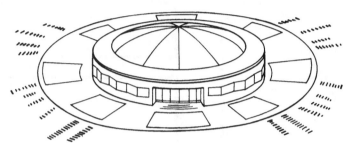

	Number of Seats	Cost per Seat	Maximum Profit
Section A		x $80	
Section B		x $60	
Section C		x $25	
Section D		x $20	
Section E		x $15	
Totals	50,000		

Stadium Proposal *(cont.)*

Directions: Use the data from the chart on the previous page to assign each section below with the letters A, B, C, D, and E to show each section of the stadium you are designing. Write a brief summary explaining why some sections are larger than others. Cite your data from the chart.

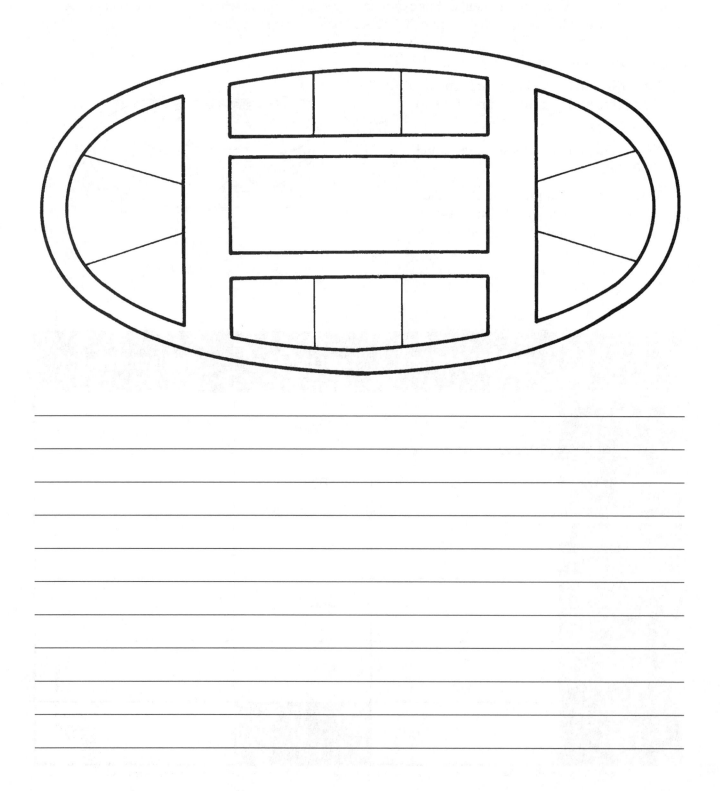

_____

_____

_____

_____

_____

_____

_____

_____

_____

_____

_____

Descriptive Writing

Magazine Mania

Making News

A Piece of Realia

About Time

A Welcome Burial

Another World

Sight Unseen

Love Is In the Air

Alliteration ABC

Figuratively Speaking

Angles and Such

Mystery Object

Radical Rocks

Unequivocally News

Nature Takes a Hike

Magazine Mania

Students use magazine pictures to describe an event or memory using creative thought and language. For example, a picture of some children running through a sprinkler on a warm summer day might remind the students about popsicles and watermelon. They then cut out the picture, secure it to the space on their papers, and use descriptive language to write about the scene in the picture. Post the students' work on a bulletin board, or combine their pages to make one memorable book for them to look at in their spare time.

Materials

- activity sheet (page 97)
- scissors
- magazines
- glue

Standards and Benchmarks: 1A, 1E, 1F, 1H, 1J, 2A, 2C

Making News

Every holiday, new vocabulary word, or story character will have special meaning when students use these terms to create headlines related to the words. Each letter of the word becomes the first letter of the next word in the headline.

Following their visual headline, encourage more descriptive writing by having the students create short news stories that coincide with their headlines.

Examples

Man **A**ttacks **N**apkin **I**n **A**ffluent **C**lub
Winning **I**dol **L**eads to **B**asic **U**nalienable **R**ights

Materials

- activity sheet (page 98)

Innovation on a good idea

Students may wish to apply their word-processing or desktop-publishing skills by electronically creating their own news reports with headlines. Depending on the software available to your students, they may import and center their headlines, then design newsletters with two or three columns. They may even wish to add graphics, scanned images, or digital-camera images to their newsletters to create authentic-looking reports.

Magazine Mania

Directions: Look through a magazine and find a picture that reminds you of something else. For example, a picture of some children running through a sprinkler on a summer day might make you think of popsicles and watermelon. Cut out the picture and glue it in the space provided. Then write a descriptive paragraph or essay describing what is happening in the picture, including the thoughts that come to mind when you look at this picture.

_____

_____

_____

_____

_____

Making News

Directions: Use a new vocabulary word, holiday term, or character name to write a newspaper headline that has to do with the word. (See the example below.) Write the letters of the word first. Leave enough space between the letters to write words. Then use them as the first letter of each word in the headline. You may simply add in words such as "a," "an," and "the," if needed. Write a news article to accompany your headline.

Maniac: **M**an **A**ttacks **N**apkin **I**n **A**ffluent **C**lub

EXTRA! EXTRA!

WEDNESDAY	• FRONT PAGE •	NEWS

A Piece of Realia

What better way to get students to write descriptively than to give them a piece of the real thing and describe it! With this activity, students use aesthetic art supplies (e.g., felt, fur, feathers, sand, etc.) to create an original collage or picture, then use descriptive language to write about their creations. Students have the option of creating a flat image on their activity sheet, or making a three-dimensional object about which to write.

Materials

- activity sheet (page 100)
- glue
- scissors

- miscellaneous art supplies such as feathers, felt, pipe cleaners, fur, sand, glitter, etc.

About Time

Students may stretch their imaginations and utilize their descriptive language skills by creating a brochure describing life in the future. They should consider the physical objects that might change in appearance (building, toys, food, furniture, etc.) as well as the intangibles (government, society, etc.). Then they can create tri-fold brochures describing this new and exciting life that awaits mankind.

Materials

- activity sheet (page 101)
- blank paper

A Piece of Realia

Directions: Use art supplies such as felt, feathers, or sand to create an original picture or collage in the space below. Then use descriptive words to write about the image you created.

_____

_____

_____

_____

Name _____ Date _____

About Time

Directions: For those people who are looking forward to the future, create a brochure filled with descriptions sure to entice anyone living in the present to await anxiously for the pleasures to come. Use this form to generate ideas. Use the back to continue, if you need more room. Then fold a sheet of blank paper into thirds to create a tri-fold brochure. Include only a title and vivid picture on the front cover. Explain each of the following items within the folds of the brochure.

The Things Around Us

Toys _____

_____

Buildings _____

_____

Schools _____

_____

Food _____

_____

Furniture _____

_____

Our Way of Life

Government _____

Entertainment _____

Communication _____

Other Important Facts

_____

_____

_____

_____

_____

_____

A Welcome Burial

Teachers who are desperately trying to encourage students to move beyond "good," "nice," "things," and "fun" should engage students in this "dead word" burial. First, enlarge the coffin and tombstone patterns on page 103 to use on a "Dead Word" bulletin board. Then have the students work in groups to think of more creative ways to write what they want to write besides the usual. The usual words are placed on the tombstones which sit above the buried coffin on the student activity page. Use the blank coffin and tombstone patterns to engage students in this activity (perhaps as a class next time) each time you encounter words in their writing which could be more descriptive.

Following their brainstorming session, allow students to practice their new talent with the activity sheet on page 105.

Materials

- enlarged coffin and tombstone pattern for bulletin board (page 103)
- additional coffin and tombstone patterns, as needed (page 104)
- activity sheet (page 105)

Another World

Students may have daydreamed about what life would be like on another planet. Here is their chance to describe this experience in a flip book designed to encourage even the most skeptical of space travelers that life on this planet would be just grand!

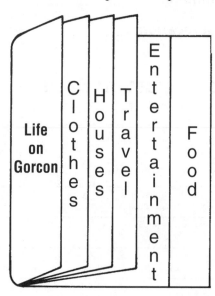

First help students fold their blank pages following the diagram to the right. Booklets should be held with the binding to the left so the pages turn to the left. Students may use the activity sheet to guide their ideas for their project. They then transfer their information, using descriptive language and vivid pictures, to the booklet. Students should label the outside edges with the title of the topic they are describing.

Materials

- three sheets of white drawing paper
  (size: 12" x 18"; 30 cm x 46 cm)
- activity sheet (page 106)

A Welcome Burial

Directions: Writing is a lot more exciting when writers use words that grab a reader's attention. Think about these "dead" words for which you might write more descriptive vocabulary. Think of more "flamboyant" ways to replace the "dead" words, and write them on the tombstones.

A Welcome Burial (cont.)

Bulletin-Board Example

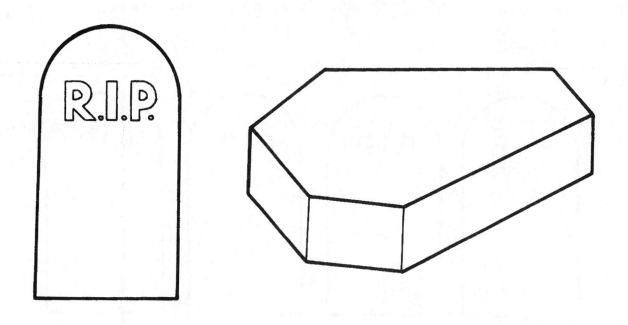

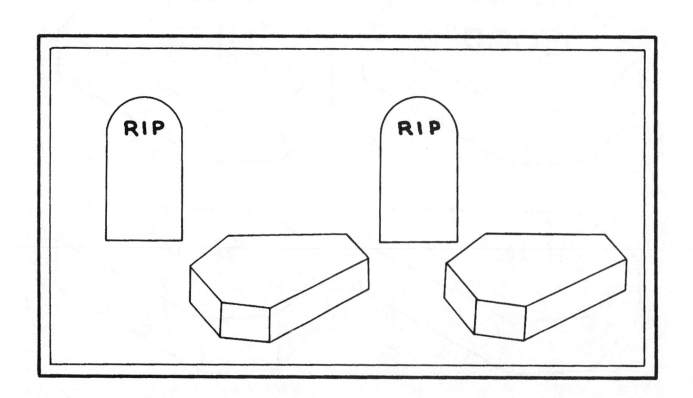

Name _____ Date _____

A Welcome Burial (cont.)

Directions: Some words such as "good" and "nice" are frequently overused by writers. Read the passage below. Find five such words to replace with more vivid language that help make the passage come alive. Cross out the words with a red pen or crayon. Write a better word in the margin. Then illustrate the passage with vivid colors.

The Day the Earth ~~Cracked~~

Margin

Split Wide Open

Once, while I was walking to school, I noticed a large crack in the sidewalk. "That's odd," I thought. "I don't remember that crack being so large." But I didn't think too much of it, and so I went on to school.

I never gave the crack a second thought until science class. We just happened to be learning about volcanoes and earthquakes and how sudden shifts in the tectonic plates might cause the Earth to shake and split. Mrs. Reynolds was just about to start her volcano model when we all suddenly felt the ground under our feet shake. It was an earthquake!

Fortunately, it didn't last very long, and the only thing that broke was the chalk when it fell from the chalkboard.

On my way home, I noticed the crack in the sidewalk was very wide. I rushed home to tell my mom. She said I should call a local cement layer. "I don't repair sidewalks," he said. "Try the City Public Works office." And so I did.

"We don't repair sidewalks," they said. "Try the County Building Division." And so I did.

"We don't repair sidewalks," they said. "Try the State Transportation Department." And so I did.

"We can't be bothered with your sidewalk," they said. "Try the U.S. Department of the Interior."

When I called them and got the same answer, I tried to explain that I think the earthquake we had was caused by this crack in the sidewalk. "Good work, young man," they said. "We will be sure to send our best seismologists to check it out."

The next day, I walked to school and found the sidewalk had been repaired. We never had another earthquake near us again.

Name _____   Date _____

Another World

Directions: Have you ever thought about what life might be like on another planet? Here's your chance to describe this experience and encourage other people to want to live there, too! First think of a name for your planet. You may select one from our own galaxy or make one up. Then consider each of the topics below. Use descriptive language to explain how these items look: their color, shape, and special features.

Life on Planet _____

The clothes are _____

_____

_____

_____

People live in _____

_____

_____

_____

_____

To get around, you might travel by _____

_____

_____

_____

For fun, you might try _____

_____

_____

The food is splendid! A meal might consist of _____

_____

_____

Sight Unseen

Advertisers use colors, language, and pictures to advertise and display their products on store shelves in an effort to get consumers to purchase their items. But what about radio announcements? The only tool advertisers may rely on is the spoken word. Engage students in this task to help them apply some of their descriptive writing talents.

Bring in a radio if your classroom does not already have one and listen for the radio advertisements (or tape some ahead of time). When they come on, have students listen critically for descriptive words and phrases as well as voice pitch and expression to determine how the advertisements entice consumers to purchase products even though the listener can't actually see them.

Provide cereal box fronts, chip labels of various flavors, can labels, or other product packaging in a brown paper bag, one for each student. Each student selects one bag and uses the contents to write a descriptive radio ad that describes the product but doesn't mention it's name. Students first use the activity sheet on page 108 to plan and write their descriptive ads. Then have the students share their work orally with the class, either by reading their works or taping them and "playing" them on the radio. Following the advertisement, the student's classmates guess the specific product that was advertised. If, after three guesses, the students still don't have the correct product, the student displays the packaging and discloses the product.

Materials
- radio (for audio advertisements)
- one product label per student
- one brown bag per student
- activity sheet (page 108)

Innovations on a good idea

Continue to encourage the students' descriptive creativity by having them develop an oral and visual ad for a product of their choice. Following their "radio" advertisements the students' classmates guess the products and the students share their visual aids. Display their visual ads in the hallway or on a bulletin board.

Have the students compare the pros and cons of radio, newspaper, and television advertisements. Discuss how descriptive language pervades each method of advertising.

Name _____ Date _____

Sight Unseen

Directions: You've been asked by your boss to write a radio advertisement for a familiar product. The only catch is, you can't mention the product's name! Your goal is to sell this product for your boss, so you should describe the product in great detail so the consumer just can't pass it up! Start by thinking about the different aspects of the product. Remember, too, that figurative language and exclamations like "Wow!" "Pop!" or "Vroom!" are effective ways of getting a listener's attention. Then write your radio advertisement below.

Think about . . .

❏ how it looks   ❏ what it's used for

❏ how it benefits people   ❏ why it's important

❏ how it tastes   ❏ when you'd use it

❏ how it makes you feel   ❏ how it's used

_____

_____

_____

_____

_____

_____

_____

_____

_____

_____

_____

_____

_____

_____

Love Is In the Air

For an extra special and descriptive Valentine's Day message, have students think of some very heartfelt descriptive words and write them in little heart shapes. Students first brainstorm some appropriate words that relate to Valentine's Day, love, or friendship. (You may wish to copy the activity sheet onto pink copy paper.) Then they use their heart shapes to write a story with a Valentine's Day theme using their heartfelt descriptive words.

Materials

- activity sheet (page 110)
- candy hearts (optional)
- pink copy paper (optional)
- glue

Innovation on a good idea

Another option is to have students respond to one of the story starters and, instead of including their descriptive words, have them glue little candy hearts with appropriate messages in strategic locations within their writing. Either way, the students' Valentine's Day stories will be genuinely descriptive.

Standards and Benchmarks: 1A, 1E, 1F, 1H, 1J, 2A, 2C, 3D, 3E, 3F, 3G

Alliteration ABC

With this activity students can practice their descriptive language skills and parts of speech while providing younger learners with a visual to help them learn their ABCs. Assign each student (or pair of students, if need be) a letter of the alphabet. They use the activity sheet to plan a descriptive sentence where each word starts with the letter they are assigned.

Example:

Betty Buffalo baffled Big Bird.

Then they transfer their sentence to a word processor, print, and illustrate their sentence. Bind all the pages in alphabetical order and have each student, in turn, visit a kindergarten or first grade classroom where he or she may share the book with a small group of younger students.

Materials

- activity sheet (page 111)
- printing paper
- word-processing software
- drawing materials

Name _____ Date _____

Love Is In the Air

Directions: Write a special Valentine's Day story with descriptive, heartfelt words. First, think of some creative words related to Valentine's Day, love, or friendship. Write them in the heart shapes below. Cut out the shapes and use them in your story. You may select one of the story starters below or think of a story on your own. Write your story on a separate sheet of paper.

Valentine's Day Story Starter Titles

❏ A Day In the Life of Cupid

❏ The Cutest Frog

❏ The Bunny Who Loved His Honey

❏ A Special Day

❏ The Day Butch the Bully Showed He Cared

❏ The Misguided Arrow

Name _____ Date _____

Alliteration ABC

Directions: Use this page to help you organize your thoughts as you create an alliterative sentence for one letter of the alphabet. Brainstorm a list of words that start with that letter. Think of several words for each of the parts of speech listed below. Then create three descriptive sentences, using the words you wrote. Type your best sentence into a word-processing program. Print your page and illustrate your sentence.

Nouns	Verbs	Adjectives	Adverbs

Write three alliterative sentences using the words you wrote.

Example: *Betty Buffalo baffled Big Bird*

1. _____

_____

2. _____

_____

3. _____

_____

Figuratively Speaking

Students will take to writing figuratively like flies to honey when they practice this element of writing while including some vivid illustrations. Share some figurative language, or distribute copies of *Mad As a Wet Hen!* to each student. (Other good resource books include ones written by Fred Gwynne. See the list of resources below.) Introduce the use of figurative language by sharing some phrases either from the book or by introducing the phrases below and helping students identify situations in which they might be used. Then share the illustrations on the following page with the class and have them identify the familiar phrases that accompany them. If they can't guess by using the picture, help them by sharing the accompanying sentences. If they still can't guess, give them the answer.

Next, have students either select a phrase from the book or one of their own favorites for which to create a three-part study card. Give each student a sheet of drawing paper measuring 4" x 12". They fold the paper to make three boxes, each 4" x 4" in size. Then they write the figurative phrase in the first box, a picture illustrating the literal meaning in the second box, and the phrase's meaning in the third box. Have each person in turn fold back the two worded ends so that only the picture is showing. Then he shares the center of his card as the class tries to guess the figurative phrase. Once this is disclosed, he shares what the phrase really means. You may wish to challenge the class to use the phrase in a sentence. Post the students' work on a bulletin board entitled "Figuratively Speaking."

For more practice using figurative language in their writing, have students complete the activity sheet on page 114 and select one of the sentences for which to write a story. They should include a literal picture to demonstrate the use of the figurative language they selected.

Sample Figurative Language Phrases

❏ Don't bite the hand that feeds you.

❏ Kill two birds with one stone.

❏ A bird in the hand is worth two in the bush.

❏ Never look a gift horse in the mouth.

❏ You can't teach an old dog new tricks.

❏ The early bird gets the worm.

Materials

- *Mad As a Wet Hen! And Other Funny Idioms* by Marvin Terban or figurative phrase samples above
- activity sheet (page 114)
- writing and drawing paper
- figurative language resource books by Fred Gwynne

     — *The King Who Rained*

     — *The Sixteen Hand Horse*

     — *A Chocolate Moose for Dinner*

     — *A Little Pigeon Toed*

Figuratively Speaking *(cont.)*

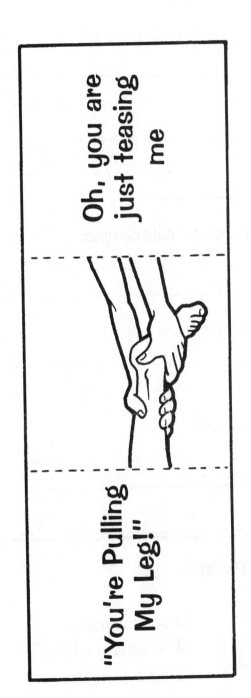

Oh, you are just teasing me

"You're Pulling My Leg!"

Now I am in really big trouble!

"I'm up the creek without a paddle!"

Name _____ Date _____

Figuratively Speaking

Directions: Read each of the sentences below. Rewrite them using a more figurative phrase. Use the phrase box below to help you. Then select one sentence to include in a story. Illustrate your story with a literal picture of the phrase. For example, if you were writing that you "heard the news right from the horse's mouth," your illustration would show you talking to a horse.

1. "I'm coming! I'm coming!" I replied when my friend asked me to hurry.

   _____

   _____

2. My older brother always has to know what I'm doing with my friends.

   _____

   _____

3. Sarah couldn't help but feel a little jealous of Jenny's gold necklace.

   _____

   _____

4. I threatened my little sister not to tell our secret, but she did.

   _____

   _____

5. Learning how to use a computer couldn't be easier.

   _____

   _____

Figurative Phrases

❏ stick your nose in other people's business

❏ a piece of cake

❏ spill the beans

❏ green with envy

❏ hold your horses

Angles and Such

Today's "new math" seems filled with an abundance of specific vocabulary the students not only are supposed to know but also use to describe and explain. This activity will help them do both. Duplicate a copy of the geometry shapes on page 117 for each student or use a poster printer to enlarge it for the class. Students use it as a resource to draw a figure using five of the shapes on the activity sheet. They may also include other vocabulary you wish to reinforce (such as curved line, 90° angle, closed plane figure, etc.). Then they write a description of how the figure should be made. Pair up the students. Have one partner read his description while the other attempts to draw the figure. (The reader hides his paper so the drawer can't see it until the end.) Then they switch places, and the drawer becomes the reader. At the end, the students share their drawings and compare them to the ones the readers had made. As a class, discuss how this activity might help the students become better descriptive writers (and critical listeners).

Materials

- geometry resource (page 117) • activity sheet (page 116)

Standards and Benchmarks: 1A, 1B, 1C, 1D, 1E, 1F, 1G, 1J, 2A

Mystery Object

Students may develop their descriptive writing skills by writing to describe a mystery object to their classmates. Collect a random sampling of the items listed below. Place them in plain brown paper bags to disguise their identity. Distribute a bag to each student or pair of students. (Some students may have the same object. The class may find comparing the two descriptions interesting following this activity!) Students use the activity sheet to first organize their thoughts, then write their descriptions. Allow time for the students to orally share their writings and have the class guess what's in their bag. Post the brown bags and descriptions on a bulletin board entitled "What's In the Bag?"

Materials

- items below • brown bag for each student • activity sheet (page 118)

Items for the "Mystery Bag"

❑ empty spool	❑ emery board	❑ napkin
❑ paper clips	❑ ball of yarn	❑ buttons
❑ cotton balls	❑ sheet of tinfoil	❑ toy block
❑ small teddy bear	❑ cotton swabs	❑ dried leaves
❑ plastic fork, knife, and spoon	❑ eye dropper	❑ ribbon

Name _____ Date _____

Angles and Such

Directions: Create an original geometric by connecting five geometric shapes. Then write a paragraph describing how to draw the figure you made.

Angles and Such *(cont.)*

Use these geometric shapes, as well as additional line segments, angles, and other pertinent geometry vocabulary to create your figure and decribe it.

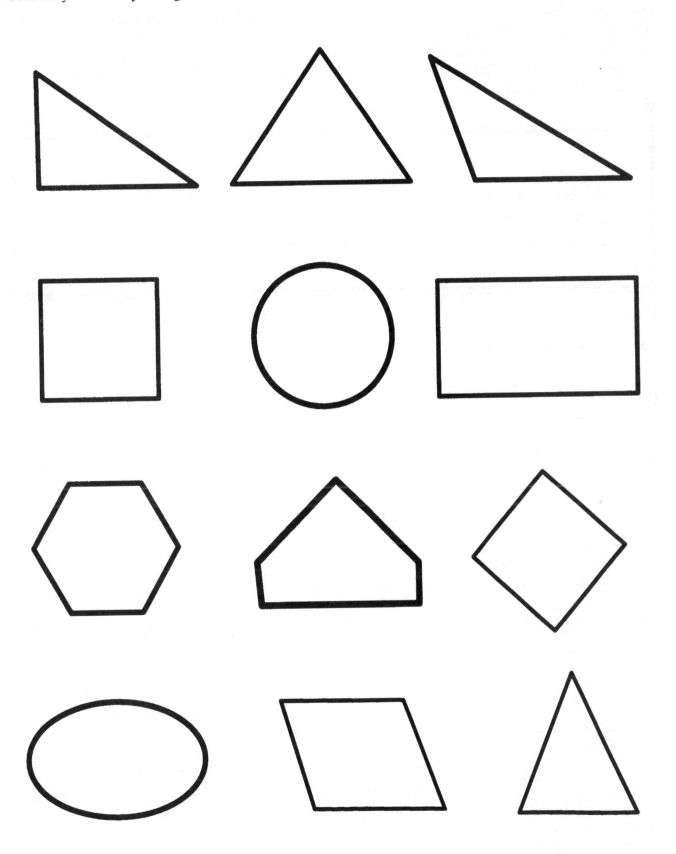

Name _____ Date _____

Mystery Object

Directions: Have you ever tried to envision an object someone was describing to you but that you had never seen? Were their descriptions good enough so that you pictured the object correctly? Here's your chance to develop descriptive writing skills using a mystery object. First think about the different ways you might describe this object, then write a descriptive paragraph as if you were the object so others may guess what you are.

Things to think about . . .

❑ How is it shaped?   ❑ How is it used?

❑ What color(s) is it?   ❑ Can you crumple it?

❑ How does it feel?   ❑ If so, will it return to its original shape?

Can you guess what I am?

_____

_____

_____

_____

_____

_____

_____

_____

_____

_____

Radical Rocks

Young geologists will be eager to describe their new and sensational finds once they mold, mesh, and form a new rock formation. Follow one of the recipes below or try visiting the Web site for more play-dough recipes. Use the parent letter on page 121 to ask parents to support you with this project. Mix the ingredients ahead of time and place the resulting dough at an art table along with the "extras." Students first use the dough and other materials to create a new rock formation, then use what they learned about geology to identify its class and describe its physical make-up as well as where it was found and why it's such an important discovery! Encourage students to use geology terms in their descriptions. Then create a geological (but temporary) display of all the students' rocks and descriptions. Allow time for students to share their discoveries before they eat them (if using an edible recipe).

Materials

- ingredients below
- parent letter (page 121)
- wax paper
- student activity sheet (page 120)

Recipes

Peanut Butter Dough

- 3 ½ c. (.83 L) creamy peanut butter
- 4 c. (.95 L) powdered milk
- 4 c. (.95 L) powdered sugar
- 3 ½ c. (.83 L) corn syrup

Oatmeal Dough

- 2 c. (.47 L) creamy peanut butter
- 2 c. (.47 L) powdered milk
- 2 c. (.47 L) rolled oats
- ⅔ c. (158.8 mL) honey

Extras:

- ❏ sprinkles
- ❏ colored sugar
- ❏ raisins
- ❏ peanuts
- ❏ chocolate chips
- ❏ colored candies
- ❏ coconut
- ❏ crisp rice cereal
- ❏ red hots

These and other "make it yourself" play dough recipes may be found under "Recipes" at
The Buddy Pages: *http://www.geocities.com/Heartland/Acres/7875/index.html*

Innovations on a good idea

If edible play-dough rocks aren't feasible, students may use clay, sand, pebbles, bark, dried leaves, or other natural materials to create their rocks.

Radical Rocks

Directions: You are a geologist out rock climbing and cave exploring when you come across a rock that you have never seen before. This is an exciting find! You collect your sample and rush back to your lab where you may study the rock more closely and identify its class. Draw and color this new rock in the box below. Then use some geology terms to describe why you classified it as you did, where you found it, and why it's such an important discovery.

Radical Rocks (cont.)

Use this parent letter to support the "Radical Rocks" activity on page 120.

Radical Rocks!

Dear Parents,

We will soon be making and writing about new and exciting rock formations. But we need your help! Please support our learning efforts by contributing the following materials. Thank you for your time and consideration.

Sincerely,

_____
Teacher

We are in need of (ingredient) _____ on or before

(date) _____ for our activity.

✂ -

(Cut on dotted line and return lower portion.)

Parent _____

Student _____

❑ Please check and return by (date) _____
    if you are unable to contribute at this time.

Unequivocally News

Students will "frantically" use "fascinating" adjectives and adverbs when they identify them in an interesting news article, chart them on the student activity page, and use them to write a descriptive narrative of the article they read. Following this "aggressive" fact-finding and creative writing activity, allow the students to type their narratives in a word-processing program, then highlight the adjectives and adverbs using one of a variety of font effects (for example, bold, outline, italics, etc.). Students may then print their papers to "proudly" post on a creative-writing bulletin board.

Materials

- news article for each student
- student activity sheet (page 123)
- writing paper
- word-processing program

Nature Takes a Hike

Nature has a beauty all its own, regardless of how it is viewed. Students use three of their five senses to log sights, sounds, and smells they experience in nature and then use their descriptive writing talents to write a related story. First, select an appropriate day when students may fully appreciate the out-of-doors. Place the students in strategic locations around the school building or on the nature trail, all within sight of you. Their only task while they are outside is to sit and listen, see, and smell for about five minutes. They use the chart on the student activity sheet to record their sensory observations. Collect the students and return to class. If desired, you may have the students pair up to share their observations, then ask each pair to share one or two things they had in common with the rest of the class. Using their descriptions, have the students use writing paper to write stories about their experiences while hiking in the woods. Allow them to rewrite their stories on parchment paper or type them in a word-processing program and print them on parchment paper; then do a few leaf rubbings around the edges to give them a more "woodsy" look. Bind the students' work to create one class book of nature stories to place in the Media Center.

Material

- activity sheet (page 124)
- parchment paper (optional)
- book-binding materials
- writing paper
- word-processing program (optional)
- leaves and crayons (for leaf rubbings—optional)

Name _____ Date _____

Unequivocally News

Directions: Read an interesting news article from a local paper. As you read, identify the adjectives and adverbs, and then identify the nouns and verbs or adjectives they describe. Log your findings in the chart below. Then, on the back of this paper, write a story with the problem in the article as the problem in your story. Include detailed events leading up to the solution you read about in your article. Use the adjectives and adverbs you identified in your story.

Adjective	Noun It Modifies		Adverb	Verb or Adjective It Modifies

Name _____   Date _____

Nature Takes a Hike

Directions: Step outside on a sunny day and get in touch with nature. Sit for five minutes and record the sights, sounds, and smells you observe around you. Use these ideas in a story about a time you went hiking in the woods. Begin your story on the lines below. Continue your story on the back of this paper, if necessary.

Sights	
Sounds	
Smells	

_____

_____

_____

_____

_____

_____

_____

Poetry

At the Ballgame

Out of the Box

Bang!

Birds of a Feather

Spring

Happiness Is Haiku

A Shapely Poem

A Card For All Occasions

Kites

All About Autumn

Native Expressions

At War

At the Ballgame

Following a class reading of "Casey at the Bat" and class singing of "Take Me Out to the Ballgame," challenge students to write their own verses for America's favorite pastime. First, help the class get started by brainstorming a list of baseball-related terms and ideas. Students may then use the activity sheet on page 127 to write their poems.

Following the paper/pencil version of their work, have the students type their poems in a word-processing program and import baseball graphics to accompany their verses. Print and mount them onto a slightly larger sheet of construction paper and bind them to create one class book of poems.

Materials

- poem: "Casey at the Bat"
- song: "Take Me Out to the Ball Game"
- chart paper or chalkboard
- activity sheet (page 127)
- word-processing program
- clip-art software
- printing paper
- construction paper
- book-binding materials

Out of the Box

This activity will help students not only create poems but also see them in a whole new dimension. First, distribute the activity sheet on page 128, which has the pattern for a three-dimensional cube. On the six squares, students write two nouns, two verbs, and two adjectives. You may wish to encourage students to include past vocabulary words or utilize their dictionary and thesaurus skills. Students then roll their die and use the words that face up to create a poem. Another option is to have the class work in cooperative groups or at a center. They roll the dice and use the upward-facing words as the start of a poem. They should try to use one of the nouns, verbs, and adjectives in the first verse. If no nouns are showing, they select the verb and adjective they wish to use and re-roll the other dice until a noun faces up.

Materials

- activity sheet (page 128)   • scissors   • glue

At the Ballgame

Directions: Think about some words, phrases, or ideas that come to mind when you think of baseball. Write them on the back side of this paper. Now use your ideas to write a baseball poem in the diamond shape below. Your poem may or may not rhyme, and it should be at least eight lines or two stanzas long.

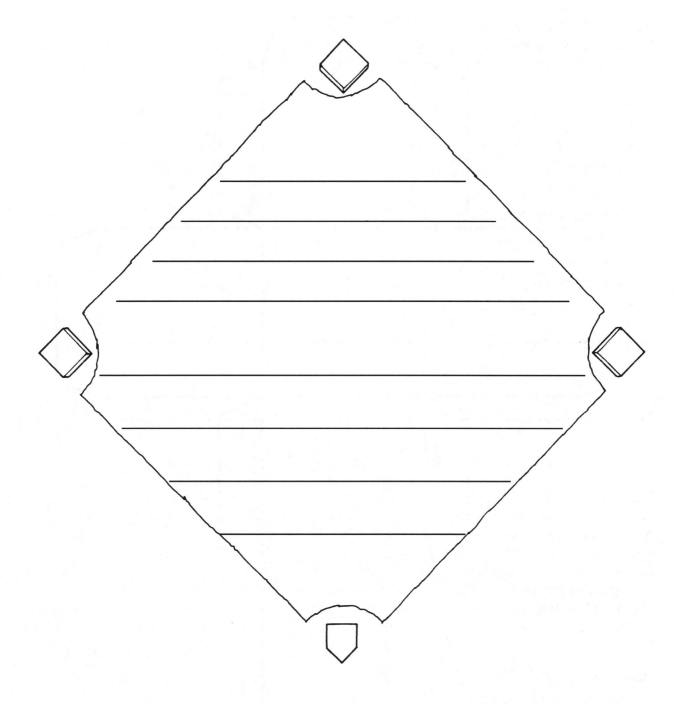

Name _____   Date _____

Out of the Box

Directions: Sometimes you may have trouble thinking of ideas for a poem. Use this cube shape to help you generate some ideas for a very unique poem. First, write one noun in each of two squares. Then do the same for two verbs and two adjectives so all the squares have a word inside them. (Your words should be extraordinary, such as *menagerie* (n.), *froth* (v.), or *ingenious* (adj.). Then cut out the shape and fold on the dotted lines to make a cube. Glue or tape sides, if necessary. Roll your cube several times and use the words that face up to write your poem.

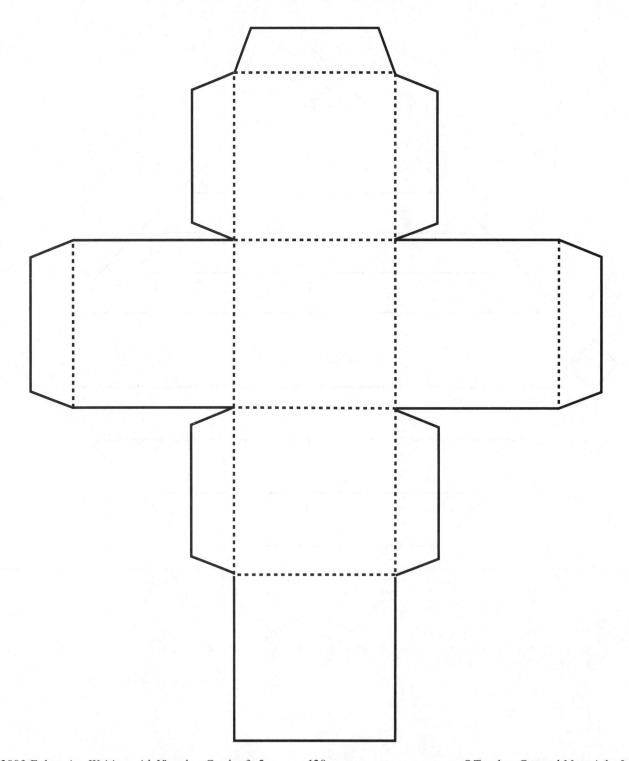

Standards and Benchmarks: 1A, 1B, 1C, 1J, 2A, 3B

Bang!

The use of onomatopoeia can enhance any writing, especially poetry. After defining this term (and practicing its pronunciation a few times), create a class list of words that fit this category of language. Then have the students write a poem about one of the themes listed on the students activity sheet where they may practice including onomatopoeia in their work. Have them write their onomatopoetic words with all capital letters to show their location in their written work. Then allow students to practice their word-processing skills by typing their poems and bolding the words to highlight them.

Materials

- chart paper or chalkboard
- activity sheet (page 130)

Standards and Benchmarks: 1A, 1B, 1C, 1J, 2A

Birds of a Feather

Colorful plumage and colorful language are the goals of this creative poetry activity. As a class, have students think about what they know about birds. If they could write a poem about any one bird, which would they choose, and why? Allow time for the class to share their thoughts. Then give them time to complete the activity sheet on page 131. Students write each line of their poem on colored sheets of construction paper, then glue them to form the bird's tail feathers. For students who write more extensive poems, they may attach some of their lines as wing feathers, as well. Create a colorful bulletin board with the students' finished products.

Materials

- activity sheet (page 131)
- colored construction paper pieces measuring 9" x 3"
- glue
- scissors

Innovations on a good idea

You may wish to complete this activity following a unit on animals, their habitats, or the rain forest.

Name _____ Date _____

Bang!

Directions: Onomatopoeia are words that sound like their meanings, such as *bang, pop, gulp,* or *beep.* Think of some more words that fit this category of language. Then choose one of the topics below to write a poem about. Include at least three onomatopoetic words in your poem.

Onomatopoeia Word Bank

- bang
- pop
- gulp
- beep

- _____
- _____
- _____
- _____

- _____
- _____
- _____
- _____

Poem Topics

- The Wild Animal
- At the Airport
- Around the House

_____

_____

_____

_____

_____

_____

_____

_____

_____

_____

_____

_____

Birds of a Feather

Directions: Think of a bird about which you would like to write a poem. Write the kind of bird you chose on the line beside the bird. Write your poem on the back of this paper. Cut and trace the feather patterns onto colored construction paper. Cut one construction paper feather for each line of your poem. Write each line of your poem on each feather. Organize them on the tail of the bird below in order from beginning to end. Color the bird.

_____

Spring

Springtime typically brings rain showers and a new beginning for plants and animals. Students take advantage of this poetry opportunity to share their thoughts and feelings about this subject with a visually appealing project. Distribute the activity sheet on page 133. First, have the students brainstorm what comes to mind when they think of this season. Next, have them use their ideas to write a free-verse poem about this topic in a "springtime-colored" crayon (such as yellow, orange, or pink) on the lines provided. Following their writing, have the students take turns at the painting table, where they will wash over their paper with a contrasting watercolor. Allow time for the papers to dry, then mount them onto colored construction paper. Bind them into one book, or display them on a springtime bulletin board. (Another option is to have students transcribe their poems onto white construction paper, then paint.)

Materials

- activity sheet (page 133)
- watercolors
- crayons
- construction paper

Standards and Benchmarks: 1A, 1B, 1C, 1J, 2A

Happiness Is Haiku

This poetic form will take on new meaning for students when they visually enhance their haiku poems with letters made from black brush strokes. First, instruct the students as to the format of these poems. Share some haikus from a book or visit the Internet to learn more about it and read some examples. Then have students try their own haiku poems, using the activity sheet on page 134. Following the writing session, they each visit the painting table where they use a thin brush and black watercolors to print their poems on a sheet of manila drawing paper; light-colored parchment paper; or rice paper, if available. Display the students' work on a special poetry bulletin board.

Materials

- activity sheet (page 134)
- black watercolors and thin paint brush
- special writing paper such as manila, parchment, or rice paper

Haiku Web Site

MidLink Magazine—haiku examples by students:
http://www.longwood.cs.ucf.edu/~Midlink/haikus.html

Spring

Directions: Springtime means many things to many people. Think about what springtime means to you. Use the word web to brainstorm some ideas. Then write a free verse poem about spring on the lines with a "spring-colored" crayon. After you finish your poem, wash over your work with a contrasting spring-colored watercolor.

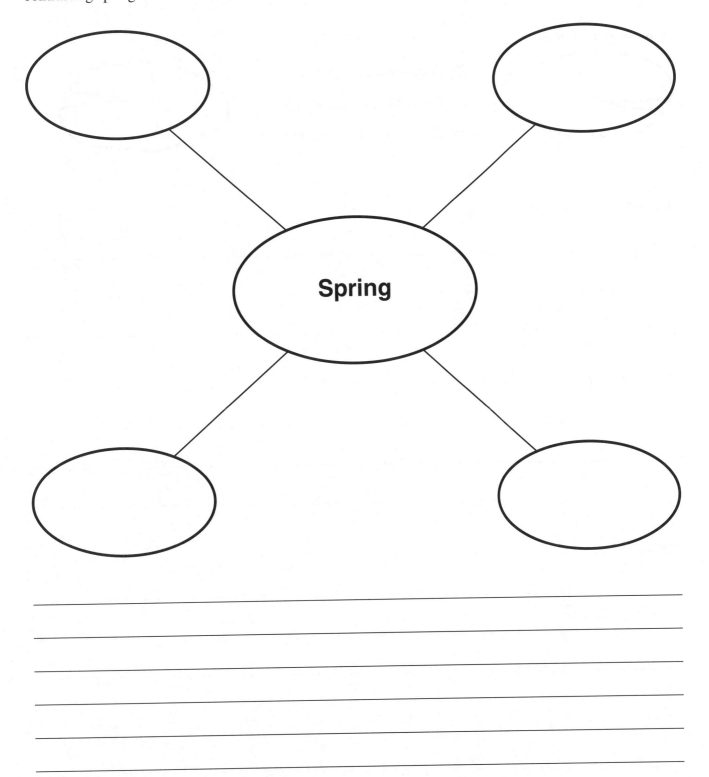

_____

_____

_____

_____

_____

_____

Name _____   Date _____

Happiness is Haiku

Directions: A haiku poem is a three-line poem, usually written about nature. Some haiku have between 10 and 14 syllables in the whole poem. Others follow a 5-7-5 syllable pattern. Read the example below. Then write three haiku poems of your own. If you have trouble getting started, think about something outside that is particularly interesting to you.

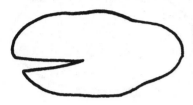

(5) Ponds with polliwogs

(7) Crickets, cattails, lily pads

(5) Chirping and croaking

Haiku #1

_____

_____

_____

Haiku #2

_____

_____

_____

Haiku #3

_____

_____

_____

A Shapely Poem

A simple yet effective way for students to express their thoughts in poetry while utilizing some effective visuals is to have them write a poem of their choosing centered around a specific topic (e.g., the rain forest, animals, ecology, etc.). Then they create a simple cutout of the shape of the topic of their poem on construction paper. For example, students writing about animals of the Southwest might choose a specific breed of snake, burrowing animal, or cactus about which to write their poems. Depending on their poems' topics, they make an outline of the shape and attach their poem to it. Once the class has finished their projects, combine all the cutouts onto a bulletin-board display of the subject the students are studying; or, mount them on uniform sheets of colored construction paper and bind them to make one class book about the subject.

Materials
- activity sheet (page 136)
- scissors
- construction paper for cutouts
- colored construction paper for book binding (optional)

Standards and Benchmarks: 1A, 1B, 1C, 1J, 2A

A Card For All Occasions

Greeting cards are filled with various sentiments; some use poetry to express the special thoughts. Bring some samples of old cards with poems on them to share with the class. (They may be specific to a holiday, if this will be the students' task.) Have student volunteers read the poems. Discuss each as a class. After they have all been read, ask the students if they have a particular favorite, and why. Explain that they will have a chance to write their own poem for a special family member or friend, either for a special occasion or just for fun. Following the students' poetry writing, they can use an electronic card-making program to create a card for the person they chose. (Students may need to be instructed or supplied step-by-step instructions as to how to use the software.) Print the poems on colored or heavier stock paper.

Materials
- old greeting cards with poems
- card-making software
- activity sheet (page 137)
- colored or heavy paper

Innovation on a good idea

For students who don't have access to a card-making program, have them word process their poems, center them, and print them on decoratively printed paper specific to the occasion. Check in your local discount or office supply store for the paper options available.

A Shapely Poem

Directions: Think about a topic you are studying in school and an animal or plant related to that topic. Write a poem about that animal or plant. For example, if you are studying the Southwest, you might choose to write a poem about a specific breed of lizard, burrowing animal, or cactus. Write the name of the animal or plant in large letters down the left side of the page. Then think of words or phrases that begin with the letters in the animal or plant's name and that also describe the animal or plant. Then cut out an outline of the shape of that plant or animal from construction paper. Glue your poem to the outline shape.

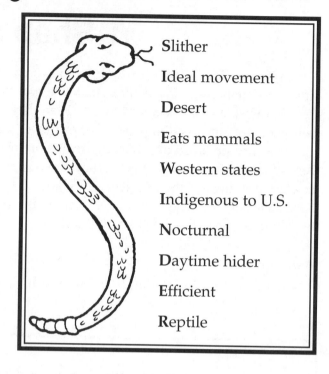

Slither

Ideal movement

Desert

Eats mammals

Western states

Indigenous to U.S.

Nocturnal

Daytime hider

Efficient

Reptile

A Card For All Occasions

Directions: People like to send greeting cards for birthdays, holidays, special events, or just for fun. Think about a reason you might send a card to a friend or relative. Write the occasion and the name of the person who will receive your card on the top lines.

Some cards have simple, short messages inside. Others send a special message in a poem. Think about the message you want to send to this person for this occasion. Write a poem for the occasion on the lines below.

This card is for _____

The special occasion is _____

Some ideas I wish to include in my poem are _____

_____

_____

_____

Write your poem here.

_____

_____

_____

_____

_____

_____

_____

_____

_____

_____

Standards and Benchmarks: 1A, 1B, 1C, 1J, 2A

Kites

Students will find freedom in poetry writing when they consider the act of flying a kite on a blustery day. First, discuss the different kinds of kites the students have seen or flown. How would they feel if they were suspended on the kite's tail or strapped to the kite itself? As a class, brainstorm a list of thoughts and ideas on this subject. Then set students to writing their poems about kite flying. They may use the activity sheet on page 139 or attach their poems to a more realistic kite they cut from a large sheet of construction paper. Give each student a length of streamer to use as a tail, and suspend the streamers from the ceiling for a breezy display.

Materials

- chalkboard or chart paper
- activity sheet (page 139)
- construction paper and streamers (optional)

Standards and Benchmarks: 1A, 1B, 1C, 1J, 2A

All About Autumn

Crisp leaves, cold noses, and biting winds might be some of the ideas that come to your students' minds when they think of this season. Encourage more thoughts by having the students think of at least eight additional ideas that are associated with autumn (see the activity sheet on page 140). Then they use the leaf pattern to trace and cut eight colorful leaves from construction paper. They write each word from their list on each of the eight leaves. Journey outside to gather thin, fallen twigs measuring about a foot long. Or, if gathering sticks is not an option, give each student a brown paper grocery bag which they cut into long thin strips (about 12" x 4") and then twist and crinkle together to make their own twigs. Students may use tape, staplers, or string to secure their colorful leaves up and down the twig. Have students sit in a large circle to share their creations and poems.

Materials

- activity sheet (page 140)
- 3"–4" pieces of construction paper in fall colors (10 per student)
- brown grocery bags (optional)
- string, tape, or a stapler

Kites

Directions: On breezy, spring days, some people think about the freedom they experience when flying a kite. Kite flying can be an exhilarating experience. But how might you feel to be an actual part of the kite itself? Think about what comes to mind when you fly a kite, or how you might feel if you could ride the kite's tail or fly suspended from the body of the kite. In the kite pattern below, write a poem about this experience. Color it, cut it out, and attach a streamer tail.

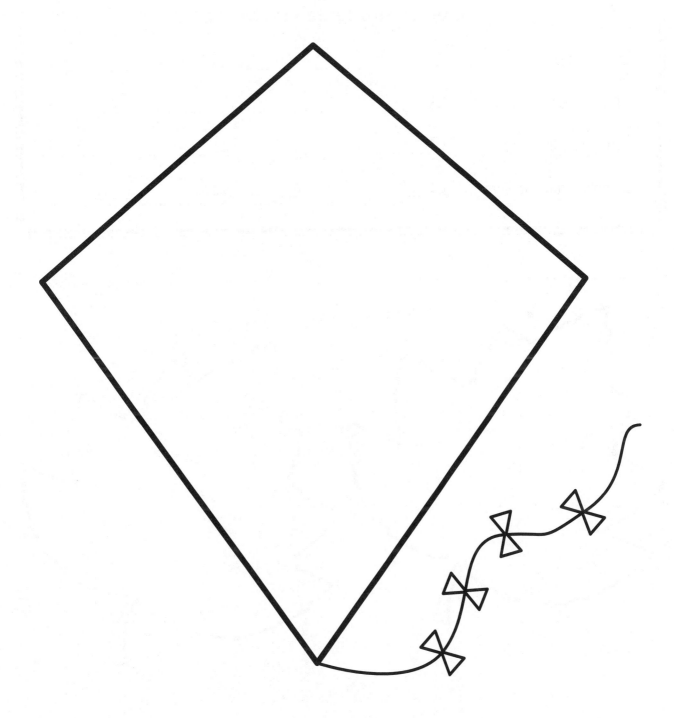

Name _____   Date _____

All About Autumn

Directions: Think about the best (and worst) parts about autumn. Write eight additional ideas on the lines below. Cut out the leaf patterns below and use them to trace and cut eight colorful leaves from construction paper in autumn colors. Write your thoughts about autumn on the leaves. Attach them to a real or fake twig.

Autumn Thoughts and Ideas

❏ crisp leaves   ❏ _____   ❏ _____

❏ cold noses   ❏ _____   ❏ _____

❏ biting winds   ❏ _____   ❏ _____

❏ chilly rain showers ❏ _____   ❏ _____

Native Expressions

Students may express their beliefs and opinions from a Native American's perspective with this poetry writing activity. Students use the activity sheet on page 142 to generate ideas and write their poems, then transfer them to parchment paper using a felt-tip black ink pen and flowing penmanship. (If the students don't have access to parchment paper, they may substitute one side of a brown paper bag that has been torn around the edges and crumpled to resemble an animal hide.) Then they collect old leaves, petals, sticks, or other "natural" elements, which they can use to decorate the border of their poems. Students may even wish to sign their work with a Native American name that describes them, followed by their given name. Arrange for the students to read their poems to a younger group of students who may also be studying Native Americans.

Materials

- activity sheet (page 142)
- parchment paper or brown paper grocery bags
- felt-tip black ink pens
- "natural" writing and drawing elements such as fallen petals, leaves, sticks, etc. (All materials should not be in use by the living plants from which they come.)

Standards and Benchmarks: 1A, 1B, 1C, 1J, 2A

At War

Teachers may really assess their students' understanding of the Civil War by following up a study of this event in American history with this poetry writing activity. First, as a class, determine the different perspectives the students may use when writing their poems. (See the list on the activity sheet for ideas.) In addition to these, your students may have other perspectives from which they might like to write a poem, or you may wish to choose the perspective of the poem depending on your focus of study. Encourage students to use descriptive words and vocabulary they may have learned during their studies. They should try to make the reader feel the anguish or elation of the situation. Following the prewriting stage (see the activity page), have the students type their poems into a word-processing program, then import graphics and/or borders from a clip-art file that enhances their work. Print the poems on parchment paper. Bind them to make one class book of Civil War poems. (Be sure to include a cover page that indicates a copyright of one of the years of the Civil War.)

Materials

- activity sheet (page 143)
- clip-art software
- book binding materials
- word-processing software
- parchment paper

Name _____ Date _____

Native Expressions

Directions: Native Americans honored the Earth and thanked her for supporting their lives. Think about what you know about the Native Americans' lifestyle and hardships. How do you think they felt while watching intruders cut down trees and kill animals for no reason? If you could share a message with those who harm the Earth, what would it be? Write a poem about nature from a Native American's perspective. Find some items from nature (not living), such as fallen leaves or petals or sticks with which to illustrate your poem with a scene from nature.

Name _____ Date _____

At War

Directions: Many Civil War soldiers kept diaries describing their experiences. Some included poems to better express their thoughts and emotions. First, decide who's perspective from which you would like to write a poem. You may choose from the list below or think of one on your own. Then think about the thoughts and feelings you wish to express as this person. Write your poem below. Include some Civil War-related drawings that have to do with the theme of your poem.

My Perspective _____

Examples

❏ soldier

❏ field nurse

❏ parent of a child at war

❏ brother or sister of person at war

❏ African-American slave

❏ African American attempting to escape on the Underground Railroad

❏ member of the Underground Railroad

_____

_____

_____

_____

_____

_____

_____

_____

_____

_____

_____

_____

_____

_____

_____

_____

_____

Bibliography

Literature

Adler, David A. *The Cam Jansen Series.* Penguin Books.

Base, Graeme. *Animalia.* Harry N. Abrams, Inc., Publishers, 1986.

Cobblestone Publishing Company. *Cobblestone.* 30 Grove Street, Suite C, Petersborough, NH, 03458.

Gwynne, Fred. *The King Who Rained.* Windmill Books, 1970.

Gwynne, Fred. *A Chocolate Moose for Dinner.* Windmill Books/Simon & Schuster, 1980.

Gwynne, Fred. *The Sixteen Hand Horse.* Windmill/Wanderer Books, 1980.

Gwynne, Fred. *A Little Pigeon Toed.* Simon & Schuster Books for Young Readers, 1988.

Ichikawa, Satomi. *Merry Christmas.* (Text by Robina Beckles Willson) Philomel Books, 1983.

Kennedy, Pamela. *A Christmas Celebration.* Ideal's Children's Books, 1992.

Kipling, Rudyard. *Just So Stories.* Henry Holt and Company, 1987.

Lawson, Robert. *Ben and Me.* Little, Brown, and Company, 1967.

Pfister, Marcus. *The Rainbow Fish.* North-South Books, 1992.

San Souci, Robert D. *The Talking Eggs.* Dial Books for Young Readers, 1989.

Sobol, Donald J. *The Encyclopedia Brown Series.* Thomas Nelson, Inc.

Terban, Marvin. *Mad As a Wet Hen! And Other Funny Idioms.* Clarion, 1987.

Thayer, Ernest Lawrence. "Casey At the Bat" from *Favorite Poems Old and New* by Helen Ferris. Doubleday, 1957.

Time For Kids. A Time, Inc. Publication. Time Life Building. 1271 Avenue of the Americas, New York, NY, 10020-1393.

Weil, Lisl. *Santa Claus Around the World.* Holiday House, 1987.

Resource Books

Blackburn, Ken and Jeff Lammers. *Kid's Paper Airplane Book.* Workman Publishing Company, 1996.

Crowley, Stewart. *How to Have Fun with Paper.* Gareth Stevens Publishing, 1996.

Editors of Klutz. *The Best Paper Airplanes You'll Ever Fly.* Klutz, Inc., 1998.

Herweck, Dona. *Write All About It!* Teacher Created Materials, Inc., 1993.

Hui, Ph.D., Edmund. *Amazing Paper Airplanes.* St. Martin's Press, 1989.

Null, Kathleen Christopher. *How to Write a Paragraph.* Teacher Created Materials, Inc., 1998.

Schmidt, Norman. *Super Paper Airplanes.* Sterling Publishing Company, Inc., 1994.

Music

Father and Daughter. "Take Me Out to the Ball Game." Available on *Diamond Cuts: A Compilation of Baseball Songs and Poetry.* Jeff Campbell. Hungry for Music. 2020 Pennsylvania Avenue, NW, Suite 384, Washington, DC 20006. *www.crosstownarts.com*

Web Sites

The Buddy Pages—*www.geocities.com/Heartland/Ares/7875/index*

MidLink Magazine—(haiku examples by students) *longwood.cs.ucf.edu/~Midlink/haikus.html.*